John Wesley for the Twenty-First Century

Set Apart for Social Witness

JOHN O. GOOCH

DISCIPLESHIP RESOURCES

PO BOX 340003 • NASHVILLE, TN 37203-0003
www.discipleshipresources.org

ISBN 0-88177-445-6

Library of Congress Control Number 2004108265

Table of Contents

Dedication

This book has been a labor of love, but it also owes a great debt to many people. Wesley scholars I never met, such as Frank Baker, Albert Outler, Manfred Marquardt, and others, have enriched my understanding of Wesley. Other scholars of Wesley with whom I have talked and worked include Richard Heitzenrater, Charles Yrigoyen, Gayle Felton, Dale Dunlap, Thomas Langford, Scott Jones, and William Abraham. I am deeply indebted to all of them for insights into Wesley's life and thought. Any mistakes, of course, are the results of my own limitations. George Donigian of Discipleship Resources suggested the direction of the book and proved a faithful and supportive editor. I am deeply grateful for his wisdom and skill.

My wife, Beth, supported my involvement in this book, and graciously blessed the time and energy I spent working on it. I owe her many days of fun and travel.

Introduction

At one time, all United Methodists (or Methodists, Evangelicals, and United Brethren) knew who we were and what we stood for. We grew up in the church and knew something about our heritage. As recently as 1938, the great majority of Methodists had been raised in that tradition. Today, a great many people who sit in United Methodist pews come from other religious traditions. They are former Baptists, Presbyterians, Catholics, or have no church background at all. They may have heard of John Wesley, but don't know anything about him. Today, even those who come from a United Methodist tradition are vague on our heritage and faith traditions. When I was in a local church, every time I announced a membership orientation class or workshop on our United Methodist tradition, I found that at least one third of the people who signed up were life-long United Methodists, but had no idea what that meant.

So when we first began talking about this book, I suggested

that it needed to answer two questions: first, "Who was this dude Wesley?" and, second, "Why should I care?" As is true of most great leaders in history, John Wesley was a fascinating and complex personality. He never intended for his followers to be anything but members of the Church of England, yet his work is the root of one of the great denominations of modern times. He was a conservative in almost all areas of his life, but also would be understood as a radical reformer. While he believed in the solid ritual of the Church, he found himself preaching out-of-doors, wherever he could gather an audience. As I began thinking about topics for the various chapters, and reading more and more by and about Wesley, I discovered (again) what a rich thinker he was. Many of his insights into life in England are incredibly relevant for life in the United States nearly 300 years later.

And why should we care? For Wesley, above all, the key to religion was found in the answer to the question, "How does one live a holy life in front of God?"(in theological terms, the search for holiness of heart and life). That key question assumed some other questions about God, Jesus Christ, salvation, but the key was always holiness. Holiness, specifically where it applies to daily life, is the key to understanding Wesley for our time. It's not just "talking the talk" about God and our relationship with God, it's also "walking the walk," taking our faith out into the family, the community, the marketplace, the larger world. How do we, as Christians, think and act about questions of education, health care, war and peace, poverty, voting, economics, and a whole host of other issues? Wesley cared deeply about those issues, not just in themselves, but because of their impact on persons created in the image of God. He calls those of us who claim to be his followers to care deeply about them as well.

John O. Gooch
Liberty, Missouri
April, 2005

CHAPTER ONE

Spirituality, Religion, and John Wesley

"I'm a very spiritual person—I just don't see any point in organized religion. What happens in church seems to get in the way of relating to God and finding my way in the world," Laura said seriously. She spent time regularly in meditation and reflection, read C.S. Lewis and other writers on the spiritual life, and felt good about what she saw as the integration of her life. She just didn't see any reason for going to church. Why bother with worship that didn't always make sense, or deal with people who were at a different place in their lives than she was? Laura felt she was a good Christian without going to church.

Sam attended Sunday School part of the time. One Sunday, in a discussion about Christianity and other world religions,

Sam blurted out, "Hey, I don't see anything wrong with being a Buddhist or following the Tao. They're all paths to the same goal. We all want to connect with God. So what's wrong with finding your spirituality in something besides Christianity? What, you think God can't handle that?"

Cynthia and Jeff loved nature. Most Sundays they were in the woods, or out on a hiking trail, or in a canoe on the river. Cynthia put it like this, "We find God in nature. Out here, it's peaceful, and no one is trying to tell someone else what to believe or how they should live. We spend the day on the river, or hiking in the forest, and we find peace. We connect with God through the natural world. Church? That seems so old-fashioned. They say the same thing every Sunday about what they believe, they pray the same prayer (which I can pray on the river) and they don't even try to get along. Why should I give up this peace I feel here—and the connection with God—to spend time in church with people I don't even know?"

"Relationships, not Religion." That's what the billboard said. It was advertising an independent congregation in the area. The message seemed to be that we can have relationships with God and with each other without having any kind of organized religion. Does that really make sense?

WAS IT IMPORTANT FOR WESLEY THAT WE BE IN CHURCH?

For Wesley, being a Christian was all about loving God with all our heart, mind, soul, and strength, and our neighbor as ourselves. And, for him, loving God and loving our neighbors meant that we banded together with other Christians to help each other live out that love. Spirituality is about loving God, which is the topic of this chapter. Loving our neighbors, also a part of our understanding of spirituality, is about making a difference in the world, which we'll discuss in chapters 3 and 5.

And, yes, it was important for Wesley that his followers be in church.

When Wesley said that the New Testament knows no solitary religion, he was drawing on hundreds of years of tradition and his own experience about how we grow in the Christian life. Some people, like Cynthia and Jeff, may be able to "find God" in nature. But the God they find there does not challenge them to grow, work for justice, or to love their neighbors. Wesley knew that being in a Christian community on a regular basis was important for his spiritual life. He needed the sense of community, the sense of being part of something more than just "me and Jesus." He needed the call to accountability the church provides—how was he doing in terms of living up to his faith commitment? We need that, too. Let's see how that worked for the first Methodists, and then take a look at how it might work for us.

The genius of the Wesleyan Revival was organization. There were other great preachers in Wesley's day, among them Jonathan Edwards in America and George Whitefield in both England and America. While all the preachers won converts to Christ through their preaching, what Wesley did differently from the others was to organize his followers into groups to both support each other and to hold each other accountable in their walk with God. That is, he put them in small groups, called classes, which were part of the society in their village or neighborhood. The society functioned like a church—for worship, preaching, the administration of the sacraments (when an ordained minister was present), and fellowship. The classes functioned as small groups that provided fellowship, opportunities for support and caring, and a time for mutual calling to accountability for the Christian life. This organization—and commitment to the community of faith—meant the Wesleyan Revival had a permanent effect on the lives of people, and on the communities in which they lived. The permanence was directly related to the common life in the community of faith, to "being in church."

Let's be clear—when we discuss spirituality in this book, we are not talking about "new age" spirituality. We are talking about a specific kind of relationship with God, with definite content. *Christian* spirituality is focused on God in Christ. It practices clearly defined spiritual disciplines, with the goal of a closer relationship with God in Christ. Spirituality is also not the same as discipleship, though they may have certain practices in common. The specific spiritual disciplines that Wesley practiced were what he called "works of piety" and "works of mercy."

WORKS OF PIETY

Wesley made it clear to his followers that being a Christian meant being actively engaged in the church. In the *General Rules*, he made it clear that anyone who was serious about her or his relationship with God would

> "[attend] upon all the ordinances of God; such are:
>
> The public worship of God.
>
> The ministry of the Word, either read or expounded.
>
> The Supper of the Lord.
>
> Family and private prayer.
>
> Searching the Scriptures.
>
> Fasting or abstinence.

Wesley referred to these practices as works of piety, or means of grace, what we might call spiritual disciplines. And here are some points about works of piety Wesley might make to Laura and Sam, Cynthia and Jeff. The heart of works of piety lies in the way we relate to the Christian community—public worship, listening to the word, and participating in Lord's Supper (Holy Communion, also known as the Eucharist). Wesley was clear that growing in faith could be done only in the community of faith, that is, the church. He expected his people to be in public worship every Sunday, and to participate in the Lord's Supper. In actual practice, many of his followers did not attend the services of the Church of England, because they were poor and illiterate, and they felt uncomfortable, if not unwelcome, in the church. But they attended regularly the preaching services when the Methodist preachers came by on their rounds, and took communion from them. They also met weekly with the class meeting, which helped them grow in their faith. In the class meeting, Wesley's followers shared their pain and struggles, helped support each other in their struggles, prayed for each other, and called each other to accountability. One of the elements of the class meeting was confession, and the members of the class would remind each other of the ways they were falling down in their commitment. The practice of accountability in Christian disciplines worked much the same way that small groups help people to stop smoking, or lose ten pounds, or exercise regularly works for us today. When we tell a group of

The *General Rules* (see page 27) are a statement about what it means to be a Methodist Christian. They were written by John Wesley himself. In addition to a brief statement about how the Methodist societies began, there is a statement about how one is admitted to the societies. The only requirement is "a desire to flee from the wrath to come, and to be saved from their sins." Then comes a list of social and economic actions that are to be avoided by Wesley's followers, a list of ways to do good to others (to love one's neighbor as oneself), and, finally, the intention to attend upon all the ordinances of God.

The *General Rules* still remain as a part of the teaching standards of The United Methodist Church.

friends that we're going to make a change in our lives and take on a new discipline, we find that it's easier to be faithful to that discipline if we know that others will hold us accountable for it.

We need to say a word about fasting as a spiritual discipline. Wesley was not interested in fasting as a way to lose weight. Fasting was a spiritual discipline, a way one might grow in holiness (see chapter 4). Wesley saw fasting as an expression of sorrow for sin, particularly for the sin of gluttony (which is not limited to food). He also saw it as a help to prayer, since the time not spent in eating could be spent in prayer. He also warned his followers not to fast if they were in poor health. Sometimes today we find youth groups engaged in a twenty-four-hour fast as a group. Going without food is intended as a way of identifying with the poor, and often involves giving money that would otherwise have been spent on food to a local food bank. This kind of fasting is done under careful supervision, with peer support, for a definite purpose, and as a way of growing in spirituality.

So Wesley might say to Laura, "You're doing a wonderful thing in your search for God and wholeness. What you lack is participation in the congregation and its life of worship, fellowship, service, and learning." He might say to Cynthia and Jeff that their quest for God was a good thing. Why didn't they share what they found with others in the church? Or, he might say to Sam that, while all faiths have the search for God at their heart, there is something unique about relating to God through Jesus Christ. We learn about that uniqueness in and through the church.

To all four, Wesley would suggest they take a look at what he called "the grand scheme of salvation," and see where they might find new ways to relate to God through Christ.

THE GRAND SCHEME OF SALVATION

Spirituality, for Wesley, was rooted deeply in what he called "the grand scheme of salvation." He was not interested in spirituality for its own sake, but spirituality rooted in God's saving acts in Christ. We can outline this "scheme" as including the doctrines of Creation, Sin, Prevenient Grace, Repentance, Justification, New Birth, and Sanctification.

Other doctrines were important to Wesley (such as the Trinity, Incarnation, Faith and Works), but these seven were the heart of his preaching and teaching. They continue as the heart of United Methodist teaching today. Other books explain these doctrines fully, a task we cannot even begin here. What we can, and will, do here is mention briefly why each of the doctrines is so important for our spirituality and our relationship with God.

CREATION

The key to the doctrine of creation for Wesley was not a literal creation in seven days, but the reality that humanity is created in the image of God. That doesn't mean we "look like" God, but that we are capable of thought, love, compassion, as well as a host of negative capabilities. We are created by the grace of God, and are called to respond to that grace. For our own spirituality, that emphasis on creation suggests that we need to remember who we are, that we are important to God, because we are created in God's own image.

SIN

We believe that we were created good (in the image of God) but our nature, at its very center, is marred and corrupted by sin. We don't like to talk about sin so much these days, but it is a present reality. Wesley believed in original sin, which means that human beings, created in the image of God, lost that image because we wanted to be the center of own lives, and to go our own way. Wesley also believed in actual sin, by which he meant a voluntary breaking of God's commandments. Sin is universal. It shows itself in our inner lives, our relationships with others, and in the social, political, and economic structures of our world. Sin, the corruption of the image of God, and the sins that result from that corruption, separate us from God and distort all parts of our lives. For us, a key part of spirituality is recognizing our sinfulness and need for God. We become more aware of this in worship, when we participate in prayers of confession, listen to the Scripture being read and preached, and search our own hearts.

PREVENIENT GRACE

Grace is a shorthand way of speaking of the incredible love of God. Wesley understood it as God's mercy that comes to us, even though we do not deserve it. It is that love that makes us right with God, gives us new life and leads us on to growth and change. Since grace is a term about relationships, it takes different forms at different stages in our walk with God. It is all one grace, one love, but it does different things, depending on our need at any particular time. Wesley (and we United Methodists) talk about those different forms of grace as prevenient, justifying, and sanctifying.

Prevenient grace is a way of talking about the reality that God loves us, even before we are aware of our need for God. "Prevenient" comes from two Latin words meaning "to go before," and describes God's love going before us, calling us, seeking us out. Sometimes prevenient grace comes to us as bad news, calling us to the awareness of our sin. Wesley sometimes referred to the bad news part of prevenient grace as convincing grace; that is, the grace that convinces us of our sin and need for God. For us spiritually, prevenient grace reminds us that sin is not the final word on human nature. We are created in God's image, we sin and turn away from God, but God always calls to us to return. We are able to face the reality of sin and confession because grace reminds us that we are already loved and forgiven by God. Now we only have to accept that grace, to say "yes" to God, and learn to forgive ourselves.

REPENTANCE

Repentance is knowing our own spiritual state, knowing that we are sinners, that we need God, that things aren't right between us and God, between us and our neighbors, and that we need God's help to make them right. Repentance is admitting we are in spiritual trouble and need help.

Both the knowing and the admitting are ways God works on us through prevenient grace. The awareness of both sin and grace leads us to repentance. This is a fresh start in our spiritual lives.

JUSTIFICATION

Justification is a legal term used in the Bible to talk about how God through Christ makes us right with God. Justification is about salvation and freedom from the guilt of sin and from the fear of God's punishment. In justification, God accepts us just as we are and changes the basic nature of our relationship with God. God's grace gives us new life and hope. This is the justifying grace that we talked about earlier.

NEW BIRTH

One of the most confusing terms in modern Christian language is "being born again." It is often used to describe a momentary, dated, experience in which we come to know that our lives have been changed by God. But not all persons have this kind of experience. So what does new birth mean for us? And does it mean that we aren't really Christians because we haven't been "born again?" Wesley says that new birth is something God does *in* us (in addition to justification, where God does something *for* us). The marks of the new birth are faith, hope, and love. We may experience new birth in many different ways, but each way is an awareness of God's grace working in and through us. A fresh start is important for our spirituality.

SANCTIFICATION

In justification, God accepts us just as we are. In sanctification, God doesn't leave us where we are. Instead, God calls us to closer and closer relationships. Sanctification (also called holiness, or Christian perfection) does not mean we never sin again, never make mistakes, or never have any more problems. Rather, in sanctification, we begin to grow toward the point where the image of God is restored in us. In sanctification, all our actions are motivated by love. Most of us will not reach this state in this life, but it is always before us as a goal, calling us to be more (in God) than we are now. In a sense, the United States Army slogan, "Be all that you can be" describes what God calls us to become. Sanctification is a fulfillment of our potential, given to us by God. Like justification, sanctification is also an act of grace. It is not something we do by ourselves, pulling ourselves up by our own spiritual bootstraps, as it were. Rather is it something God does in us, giving us grace to grow into the likeness of Christ.

Sanctification is also called holiness, the holiness of heart and life, in Wesleyan language. It is all about the life we live in front of God, growing more and more into what God calls us to become. So sanctification/holiness is the heart of our spirituality.

LIVING IN GOD'S HOUSE

In "The Principles of a Methodist Farther Explained," [*sic*] (*Works* 9:227) Wesley presents a metaphor in which he compares the life of faith to a house. Repentance, he says, is the porch of the house, justification is the door to the house, and sanctification is the whole house. The goal is being in the house, living in it, exploring all the nooks and crannies, letting it shape our lives. But in order to live in the house we have to cross the porch (repent) and enter the door (be justified, accept God's saving grace).

Picture a house in your mind, and think about how quickly you get through the door. Then think about how long you have to live in the house before you find all its hidden crannies, discover what furniture fits where, and know how you want to arrange your dishes in the cabinet, your books on the shelves, your clothes in the closet. As you begin to be comfortable in the house, you also discover that the house is making a difference in you. Who you are, how you relate to the house, and to others in it, are all changing. So it is in the life of faith.

In fact, we might push Wesley's metaphor a bit and suggest that the house is really the church. Not the building on the corner, but the community of faith. As you live in the community, and begin to find comfort in it, you discover that you are changing. You relate to God differently, you relate to others differently, you are even different yourself. This is all a part of your spirituality, which you begin to discover is not personal but shared with others.

AND SO?

We often think of spirituality as something we do, out on our own, and then bring to church. Laura, Sam, Cynthia, and Jeff all had something of that mindset. Wesley reminds us that spirituality happens in church. It happens in church because there we intentionally encounter God with the community of faith. It is in church that we hear God's word read and proclaimed. It is there that we learn of grace. It is in church that we catch the vision of the upward call of God, the call to deeper spirituality, to service, and to holiness.

QUESTIONS FOR REFLECTION

1. Why did Wesley expect his followers to participate in both the services of the Church of England and the work of the Methodist societies and class meetings? Why do you participate in the life of the church?

2. Spirituality is rooted in the "grand plan of salvation." How is that true for you? How would each element in that "grand plan" enrich your spiritual life?

3. How would you understand Wesley's metaphor of the house as a model for your own spiritual life?

4. Read aloud or sing "Come, Sinners, to the Gospel Feast" (#339 in *The United Methodist Hymnal*). How does this hymn help you understand Wesley's perspective on faith?

FOR FURTHER READING

Gregory S. Clapper, *As If The Heart Mattered* (Nashville: Upper Room Books, 1997).

Scott J. Jones, *United Methodist Doctrine: The Extreme Center* (Nashville: Abingdon Press, 2002). A readable survey of United Methodist teaching, which opens up both an historical perspective and ways in which that teaching affects our lives.

C. S. Lewis, *The Screwtape Letters*. While this book has nothing to do with John Wesley, it does teach us a great deal about new birth and the role of Christian community in the Christian life.

Charles Yrigoyen, Jr., *John Wesley: Holiness of Heart and Life* (Nashville: Abingdon Press, 1996). This was a study book for United Methodist Women in the 1990s, and can probably be found in many church libraries. It is a summary of Wesley's teachings of holiness and their importance for the Christian life today.

CHAPTER TWO

Walking the Talk

Every morning when Jeff drove to work, there they were. At the top of the exit ramp where he left the Interstate, there was a person holding a little sign that said "Hungry. Will Work for Food." Or, "Homeless, need help." Or, "Vietnam veteran. Homeless and Hungry." The heartbreaking part was the small children standing with the adults holding the signs. In the afternoon, when Jeff went home, another group would be at the stoplight just before he entered the Interstate. Same kinds of signs, same kinds of despair, same heart-breaking tug on his conscience. Every day, he wondered, *What do we do about this? If I gave money to every person holding up a sign, the task would be endless. Should I talk to them and direct them to the Union Mission, where serious help is available?* And Jeff wondered, *We're the richest nation on earth. What's wrong that people are going hungry?*

Nancy also thought about hungry and homeless people in her community. She wanted to do something to make a difference, so she signed up to cook and serve meals one night a week at a homeless shelter. She organized a food drive in her church, so the local food bank would have enough on hand to provide basic food for families in the community. Some of her friends wondered why she was working so hard for people who didn't do anything to help themselves. Some days Nancy wondered, *Why are people so hungry and homeless? Aren't they trying?* She talked to some of the people at the shelter and found out they were working two jobs. They just couldn't make enough to be able to provide housing for their families. They felt ashamed and beaten down, but kept on trying.

George had a large garden, raising much more than he and his family could ever eat. George found real pleasure in giving away fresh corn and tomatoes to his neighbors. But he found even more pleasure in filling large baskets with fresh vegetables and taking them to the community kitchen. In his heart, George always felt this was what Jesus would want him to do.

The youth group at Trinity United Methodist Church organized an "in-town work camp" every year during spring break at school. They went around the neighborhood, volunteering to help senior citizens and disabled persons clean up their yards after the winter, make minor repairs on their homes, paint, whatever needed doing. When people asked them why they were doing this when they could be having fun, they always said, "We're trying to be disciples of Jesus Christ. Thank you for allowing us to serve you."

Jeff, Nancy, George, and the youth group are all people you know. They are the people in your congregation and your community who are out doing good works, helping other people, trying to make a difference in their communities. They are also trying to be faithful disciples of Jesus Christ.

WESLEY AND GOOD WORKS

John Wesley believed in doing good works. All his life, he practiced the habit of charity. As a Fellow of Lincoln College, Oxford, he lived on his stipend of £28 a year, and gave away everything he earned above that amount. As the Methodist revival became more popular, Wesley was accused by his critics of becoming rich on his converts. In fact, Wesley did, finally, become rich because of his publications. Had he kept the profits from his publishing and invested them, he could have been among the wealthiest men in England. Instead, he gave away the profits, sometimes up to £1,000 a year. Henry Moore said that Wesley gave away £30,000 in his lifetime. (See Rack, p. 361) In modern United States dollars, that would be on the order of $4 million.

In addition, Wesley preached and practiced active charity. The Oxford Methodists collected money, food, and clothing for the poor as a part of their regular spiritual discipline. In fact Wesley regarded this ministry as a "prudential means of grace." This means that he saw doing good works as a way God had chosen to help Christians grow in faith and holiness. Wesley did not believe that we are saved by doing good works. Only the grace of God can save us. But he did believe that doing good works was a way to respond to the saving grace of God. Finally, Wesley knew that people are in no condition to listen to the gospel if they are hungry, cold, or without decent clothing.

The General Rules (see page 27) stressed concern for feeding the hungry and clothing the naked. In the class meetings, members brought contributions of cash, clothing, food, fuel, and medicine, which were distributed to the poor. In May of 1741, Wesley urged the London Society to bring clothes and a penny weekly to aid the poor. He introduced a loan fund, what we might call micro-loans. Loans for up to three months were interest-free. Wesley came up with the base capital from his own pocket— others administered the fund. During the first year, some 250 people were helped, primarily by paying off lenders who had loaned money at incredibly high rates of interest. Repayment of the principal provided a revolving fund to help others.

An even more important issue was finding jobs, in an economy where jobs were being cut rather than created. As often as he could, Wesley initiated work projects. At the Foundery, Wesley's headquarters in London, twelve people were hired to process cotton, and later women were employed in knitting. These were, obviously, only stop-gap measures in an economy that was becoming more and more machine driven, and mass production was driving household manufacturing out of the market. We don't know the results of Wesley's work projects, but we do know that people were suspicious of his motives and accused him of exploitation. (see Marquardt, pp. 28-29) It seems probable that, in a changing economy, these work projects could never be anything but temporary. Mass production meant that the work done in these projects could be done cheaper and easier in factories. But, for a time, people surely were helped. Not every good work we do has permanent benefits.

That brings us back to Jeff's questions, and to the questions people were asking Nancy. Why do all those good works? What difference does it make? And shouldn't people help themselves?

WHY SHOULD WE CARE? A THEOLOGICAL DETOUR

First, *why* should we do anything to minister to the poor or to do other good works? Wesley was clear that this is our Christian duty, that Christ himself had called us to feed the hungry, clothe the naked, visit the sick, and so on. Wesley expressed Christ's call by having God's love at the heart of his preaching. It is impossible to read Wesley's sermons, or the hymns of his brother Charles, without seeing the power of God's love in their lives. Charles' great hymn, "Come, O thou Traveler Unknown," (#387 in *The United Methodist Hymnal*) is an expression of the search to understand God's nature, and comes to the realization that God is Love. All of Wesley's good works were an attempt to return God's love, both to God and to neighbor. To hear the words of Jesus about loving God with all one's heart and loving one's neighbor as oneself meant, for Wesley, that there were practical consequences in the real world. This was not just a pious saying, reserved for church. It was a call to practical action. This love was the basis for all the Methodists did for the poor.

In addition, Wesley's theology was a part of the "middle way" he had learned from the Church of England. The Protestant Reformation of the sixteenth century was, in part, a reaction against what was perceived as the Roman Catholic Church's emphasis on works for salvation. This was a misunderstanding of what the church really taught, but the perception was reality for many of the continental Reformers. They thought the church was teaching that, if one just did enough good works, one could ensure her or his own salvation—and perhaps lay up a store of extra merit that would apply to the salvation of others, as well. In reacting against this "works righteousness," reformers such as Martin Luther and John Calvin insisted on the primacy of grace for salvation. Luther even used the phrase

> Grace alone
>
> Faith alone
>
> Scripture alone.

By this he meant that we are saved only by God's grace. The only thing we can do to help ourselves is to accept that grace in faith. Now Wesley agreed that we are saved by grace, and that we need to accept grace in faith. But he also wanted to keep the best from the Catholic tradition as well. So he insisted on

> Grace *and* Faith
>
> Faith *and* Works
>
> Scripture *and* Tradition, Reason, and Experience.

In Chapter 1, we talked briefly about grace and faith. In Chapter 15, we'll talk about how Wesley interpreted Scripture. For now, we want to focus on faith and works. We are saved by grace through faith, Wesley preached. But we are then called to express that faith in good works. What we do is an expression of who we are. And, if we are really Christian, we express our faith and respond to God's grace in what we do for our neighbor. That's *why* we do good works. It's a part of the continuing quest for holy living that Wesley stressed throughout his life.

WHAT CAN ONE PERSON DO?

So, second, *what* do we do about loving our neighbors? *How* do we express God's love by our actions in the world? Wesley's model—and the biblical model as well—would suggest that love is more than an emotion, or a vague, generalized way of feeling about our neighbors. His model would suggest that love is a tough, hands-on, caring for people who may not care for us. Wesley's model would lead us to be active in feeding the hungry, clothing the naked, housing the homeless, providing medical care for those who need it and can't afford it, visiting the sick, visiting prisoners, and so on.

In addition, Wesley emphasized personal contact with those in need. It's fine, he said, to give anonymously through institutions. Write the checks, he would say to us—they make a world of difference to people in need. But it's even better if you get involved. See with your own eyes who people are and what they need. An evening talking with persons in a homeless shelter, for example, would help get rid of some of the stereotypes we have about the poor and homeless. It might take us beyond the "Why don't they take some responsibility for themselves?" kinds of questions that Nancy was asked at the beginning of this chapter. Wesley also urged that Methodists deliver help, not send it. If we are actively involved with people in need, we can also help them to grow out of their situations. If we have a concern that our charity and good works are only perpetuating a situation, hands-on involvement may help both ourselves and the people to whom we minister to grow and move beyond their present situation.

On a personal note, I well remember the first time my family responded to the challenge to get personally involved. Without going into details, our eyes were opened. We saw what poverty and need really were, and we resolved to get involved beyond that day's Christmas gifts. Over a period of years, we were able to help a family take some steps to escaping the cycle of poverty and welfare. In the process, we developed relationships that bridged the gap between races, classes, and economic status. That was the model Wesley suggested for us.

WHAT ABOUT THE BIG PICTURE?

How do we live out God's love in an economic system that is so much bigger than anything one person can begin to grasp? Wesley was convinced that poverty was the result of clear causes. (See Chapter 8) One cause he championed was the need for a minimum wage, that would actually provide a decent living for a family. That is an issue that is still being fought out today, in Congress and other arenas. Do we need a minimum wage? What should it be? In other cases, Wesley said, unemployment was undeserved. Remember that many people were thrown out of work in England because of the advancing Industrial Revolution, just as people are thrown out of work today because of factors beyond their control. We cannot, Wesley said, justly blame people for something they can't help. This means that knowing something about the causes of unemployment and poverty, or lack of medical care, becomes an ethical issue for those who try to follow Christ.

Finally, we refer once more to The General Rules. The second part of the General Rules (see p. 27) is a guide for *how* we live out the commandment to love our neighbors in practical ways. It is not an all-inclusive guide, but it offers some important principles. And we remember that the guidelines of the General Rules are set in a context of how Methodists express their love for God and their desire for salvation.

QUESTIONS FOR REFLECTION

1. How do you feel about the question of poverty? Why do you think people are poor? Do the poor simply not try?

2. What are some theological reasons why we should care about people in physical need?

3. What can you do to minister with the poor? How can you serve with the least of God's children?

4. What can you do (or should you?) to deal with poverty on a wider scale than just your own personal giving?

5. Is it enough just to feed the hungry?

FOR FURTHER READING

Barbara Ehrenreich, *Nickled and Dimed: On (Not) Making it in America* (New York: Henry Holt and Company, 2001). A first-hand account of how the working poor in America struggle just to exist.

Theodore Jennings, *Good News to the Poor: John Wesley's Evangelical Economics* (Nashville: Abingdon Press, 1990).

Manfred Marquardt, *John Wesley's Social Ethics* (Nashville: Abingdon Press, 1992). Translated by John E. Steely and W. Stephen Gunter. This scholarly work tackles a variety of social issues and the ethical responses of John Wesley and other early Methodists. We will refer to it many times in the rest of this book.

Henry Rack, *Reasonable Enthusiast: John Wesley and the Rise of Methodism* (Philadelphia: Trinity Press International, 1989). An in-depth biography of John Wesley, set against the political, social, and economic background of eighteenth-century England

CHAPTER THREE

The General Rules of the Methodist Church

THE NATURE, DESIGN AND GENERAL RULES OF OUR UNITED SOCIETIES

In the latter end of the year 1739 eight or ten persons came to Mr. Wesley, in London, who appeared to be deeply convinced of sin, and earnestly groaning for redemption. They desired, as did two or three more the next day, that he would spend some time with them in prayer, and advise them how to flee from the wrath to come, which they saw continually hanging over their heads. That he might have more time for this great work, he appointed a day when they might all come together, which from thenceforward they did every week, namely, on Thursday in the evening. To these, and as many more as desired to join with them (for their number increased daily), he gave those advices from time to time which he judged most needful for them, and they always concluded their meeting with prayer suited to their several necessities.

This was the rise of the **United Society,** first in Europe, and then in America. Such a society is no other than "a company of men having the *form* and seeking the *power* of godliness, united in order to pray together, to receive the word of exhortation, and to watch over one another in love, that they may help each other to work out their salvation."

That it may the more easily be discerned whether they are indeed working out their own salvation, each society is divided into smaller companies, called **classes,** according to their respective places of abode. There are about twelve persons in a class, one of whom is styled the **leader.** It is his duty:

1. To see each person in his class once a week, at least, in order: (1) to inquire how their souls prosper; (2) to advise, reprove, comfort or exhort, as occasion may require; (3) to receive what they are willing to give toward the relief of the preachers, church, and poor.

2. To meet the ministers and the stewards of the society once a week, in order: (1) to inform the minister of any that are sick, or of any that walk disorderly and will not be reproved; (2) to pay the stewards what they have received of their several classes in the week preceding.

There is only one condition previously required of those who desire admission into these societies: "a desire to flee from the wrath to come, and to be saved from their sins." But wherever this is really fixed in the soul it will be shown by its fruits.

It is therefore expected of all who continue therein that they should continue to evidence their desire of salvation,

First: By doing no harm, by avoiding evil of every kind, especially that which is most generally practiced, such as:

The taking of the name of God in vain.

The profaning the day of the Lord, either by doing ordinary work therein or by buying or selling.

Drunkenness: buying or selling spirituous liquors, or drinking them, unless in cases of extreme necessity.

Slaveholding; buying or selling slaves.

Fighting, quarreling, brawling, brother going to law with brother; returning evil for evil, or railing for railing; the using many words in buying or selling.

The buying or selling goods that have not paid the duty.

The giving or taking things on usury—i.e., unlawful interest.

Uncharitable or unprofitable conversation; particularly speaking evil of magistrates or of ministers.

Doing to others as we would not they should do unto us.

Doing what we know is not for the glory of God, as:

The putting on of gold and costly apparel.

The taking such diversions as cannot be used in the name of the Lord Jesus.

The singing those songs, or reading those books, which do not tend to the knowledge or love of God.

Softness and needless self-indulgence.

Laying up treasure upon earth.

Borrowing without a probability of paying; or taking up goods without a probability of paying for them.

It is expected of all who continue in these societies that they should continue to evidence their desire of salvation,

Secondly: By doing good; by being in every kind merciful

after their power; as they have opportunity, doing good of every possible sort, and, as far as possible, to all men:

To their bodies, of the ability which God giveth, by giving food to the hungry, by clothing the naked, by visiting or helping them that are sick or in prison.

To their souls, by instructing, reproving, or exhorting all we have any intercourse with; trampling under foot that enthusiastic doctrine that "we are not to do good unless *our hearts be free to it.*"

By doing good, especially to them that are of the household of faith or groaning so to be; employing them preferably to others; buying one of another, helping each other in business, and so much the more because the world will love its own and them only.

By all possible diligence and frugality, that the gospel be not blamed.

By running with patience the race which is set before them, denying themselves, and taking up their cross daily; submitting to bear the reproach of Christ, to be as the filth and offscouring of the world; and looking that men should say all manner of evil of them *falsely,* for the Lord's sake.

It is expected of all who desire to continue in these societies that they should continue to evidence their desire of salvation,

Thirdly: By attending upon all the ordinances of God; such are:

The public worship of God.

The ministry of the Word, either read or expounded.

The Supper of the Lord.

Family and private prayer.

Searching the Scriptures.

Fasting or abstinence.

These are the General Rules of our societies; all of which we are taught of God to observe, even in his written Word, which is the only rule, and the sufficient rule, both of our faith and practice. And all these we know his Spirit writes on truly awakened hearts. If there be any among us who observe them not, who habitually break any of them, let it be known unto them who watch over that soul as they who must give an account. We will admonish him of the error of his ways. We will bear with him for a season. But then, if he repent not, he hath no more place among us. We have delivered our own souls. (*The Book of Discipline,* 1996 ed., p. 69–72)

BUT WHAT DOES ALL THAT HAVE TO DO WITH MY LIFE?

One thing we can easily see—the General Rules are about holy living. They take Wesley's metaphor of the house and begin to put some practical glass and paint and wallpaper on the framework. Anyone who wants to find salvation can become a member of the societies. But just joining is not enough. If you want to continue in the societies, you need to work on holy living.

Part of holy living is refraining from doing evil. Part of holy living is doing good. And part of holy living is worship, prayer, and other spiritual disciplines. That is, holy living, for the people called Methodist, is about all parts of our lives. Holy living is practical, ranging from writing a check to the local food bank, to not trying to get foreign purchases back into the country without paying duty, to not pushing the debt limits on our credit cards. Oh, yes, it's all there—some of it only by implication, but it's there. We need also to remember that the General Rules are not some kind of inflexible law, but rather guidelines for holy living as a part of the Methodist movement.

Another way to think about holy living is that it involves loving God with all our heart, mind, soul, and strength, and our neighbor as ourselves. (see Luke 10:25-27)

QUESTIONS FOR REFLECTION

1. As you read the General Rules, you may have thought some of them were pretty antiquated, and didn't apply to any situations we are likely to face today. Make a list of all those you feel fall into this category. Then rewrite each of these "irrelevant" rules in a way that would make them specifically relevant to our world today. This may be the most important spiritual exercise you will do this week.

2. How would your life be different if you took living out the General Rules seriously? What old habits would you have to give up? What new habits would you have to develop?

CHAPTER FOUR

Going on to Perfection— A Way of Life

"The Perfect Body you always wanted." That was the message header on the email. Perfect bodies are a major industry in the United States. Diets are big business. Even the fast-food industry went to low-carb menus (ignoring the high-fat items that were left). Donut companies lost money at an alarming rate when low-carb became the fad diet. People spend billions of dollars on health club memberships, exercise equipment, and exercise clothing, all in the search for the perfect body (or, at least, a better one than the one they now have). Obesity is now listed as a major health concern, and anorexia continues to be popular among part of the population. All in search of the perfect body!

"I don't get it. Wesley kept talking about perfection and holiness, and I can't see *he* was all that perfect. We're going to make mistakes. Isn't it human to err, according to the old saying?"

"I don't want to have anything to do with holiness. I grew up in a church where there were strict rules about what you could and couldn't do, and I don't want anything to do with that kind of holiness. Nor do I want to get involved with shouting and speaking in tongues in the worship service. So when it comes to holiness, you can count me out."

"Our pastor says that when she was ordained, they asked her, 'are you going on to perfection?' and she had to answer 'yes.' That's scary, to have to make that kind of commitment, particularly when you know you probably can't live up to it. Is that fair for the church to ask that kind of question?"

A LOOK AT SOME WORDS

All the understandings of "perfect" above have nothing to do with what Wesley meant by perfection. They are "perfectionisms," the kind of dreams that drive advertising. We're not going to get that "perfect" body by trying fad diets, or achieve complete happiness because we drive a particular kind of car. They are "legalisms," pushing the idea that if I just try hard enough, I can be perfect.

Wesley used the words "perfection," "holiness," and "sanctification" interchangeably. To him, holiness was not so much an impossible goal to be striving for, but a way of life. In some ways, sanctification (and those other words, too) meant, "How does one live as a Christian in a world where it's often hard to do that?" In both the early church and in Wesley, being perfect meant being complete, whole, becoming everything God has put within us to become. That means, in some ways, perfection is different for each one of us, because each of us has different gifts and for each of us being complete and whole looks different.

We've already talked about spirituality and doing good works. For Wesley, these were ways in which we live out what it means to be a Christian. When we practice spiritual disciplines, we deliberately put ourselves in a position where we can grow in faith, draw closer to God and to neighbor, and be open to the voice of God calling us to new directions. For example, as one person said, "Whenever I think I have my life pretty well under control, the next time I pray, God says something like, 'That's good. You're making real progress. Now, there's this other thing I've been meaning to talk to you about.'" When we practice doing good works, feeding the hungry, caring for the sick, and so on, we live out our faith in real life. Does that make us better than someone who doesn't do those things? No. But it does help us live as a Christian in the world around us.

GOING ON

We hear a lot about God accepting us just as we are. That is true. God does love us and accept us "just as we are." God does not expect us to measure up to some impossible standard of "righteousness" before God loves us. God just loves us. God accepting us just as we are is an expression of what we call "justification." Sanctification (holiness, perfection) means that God doesn't leave us where we are. Sanctification is a change that God works in us, through grace. In technical theological terms, sanctification is the cure of sin, which sets us free from the power of sin and restores us to our original nature. To use another metaphor, sanctification is a process of growth, like moving from infancy through adolescence to maturity, in which we come to be more like Christ. Or, back to the metaphor of the house, sanctification (or holiness) is living in a house, making it our own, and exploring all the possibilities of what it means to be in that particular house (in this case, the Christian community of God's love).

So what does holiness mean in real life?

Holiness means we need to grow in our relationship with God. Remember, in chapter 1, when we talked about spirituality, we talked about "works of piety," or spiritual disciplines. Those are the "exercises" we do to help us grow in faith. If we want to participate in a sport, we have to practice the disciplines of that sport, whether it's hitting a baseball or a tennis ball, or improving our backstroke. If we want to play a musical instrument, we keep practicing, over and over, until the exercises help us reach the point where we find joy in what we do. It's the same with spiritual disciplines. They keep us practicing until we reach the point where we find joy in our relationship with God.

Holiness also means we practice doing good works, as we saw in chapter 2. If spiritual disciplines help us practice our love for God, doing good works help us practice our love for neighbor. We may begin serving meals at the homeless shelter out of a sense of obligation, but if we keep "practicing," we reach the point where we see homeless persons as children of God, and find joy in our relationship with them. We may agree to teach children out of a sense of obligation, but if we keep practicing, we reach the point where we find real joy in working with those children, and we wouldn't miss it for anything. And living out our love for neighbor is yet another way we live out our love for God.

Holiness means we live as examples and mentors for others in the church. All of us remember that, when we were children and youth, there were adults in our community that we wanted to be like when we grew up. Who are we, and how do we live, that someone else might want to be like us when he or she grows up? A senior high Sunday School teacher once sent the youth out with the instruction that they had to bring back an adult who was important in helping them become a Christian. They couldn't bring people who were teaching other classes, though they could tell a story about why they wanted to bring that person. The youth interrupted adult classes and took people back to their room. Then they each talked about how the person they had brought had been important to them in learning what it was to be a Christian. That is a living example of what holiness means.

Holiness also means that we take seriously the church's ministry of teaching. Too often, we act as if Jesus did not say we were to love God with our minds, as well as heart and soul and strength. It may very well be that we don't win more people for the church because we're afraid to deal with tough questions or face difficult issues. Regardless of how one feels about the "answer," why should the church be afraid to talk about the hard questions in the "war" between creation and evolution? Or abortion? Or economic and social justice? Reading and studying about such issues, struggling with what they mean for Christian faith, are also a part of living a holy life.

BUT . . . BUT . . . BUT . . .

But what about this "going on to perfection" business? Ah, glad you asked, because Wesley did not think that only preachers should be "striving after" perfection, as another ordination question has it. He thought that all Christians should be growing in grace, becoming more like Christ in all aspects of their lives. He even believed that, at some point along this journey, all voluntary sin would disappear. He didn't believe that we would never make mistakes. (We will always do that, in many ways. We add up a column of numbers and get the wrong answer. We say something to a friend, with the best of intentions, and inadvertently hurt their feelings.) What he did mean was that we can reach a point where we never knowingly and voluntarily violate a "known law" of God. Most of us probably don't reach that point during our lifetimes, but Wesley insisted that we should be continually working toward it.

We might guess that Wesley looked at the "commandment" of

perfection the way he looked at other commandments in the Bible. He referred to them as "God's covered promises." That is, he didn't see them as commandments, as law. Rather he saw them as promises of grace. These were not things for which God was going to hold us to account. Rather, they were promises that God made to those who tried to live as Christians. Scott Jones, in his book, *United Methodist Doctrine: the Extreme Center*, lists four things in which we trust when it comes to the call to sanctification.

1. God has promised this in the Scriptures.

2. God is able to work in us what God promised.

3. God is able to do it now.

4. God does fulfill God's promises and we experience sanctification. (p. 200-201)

Sanctification is the way we live out our trust in God's promises, knowing that God would not promise that which God cannot do.

But What if We Can't?

But what if we can't live like that? What if we fail? If we make one mistake, are we doomed for life? No, because God's grace is always at work in our lives. Sanctification is the work of God in us, through the Holy Spirit. We cooperate with that work by being open to God, seeking to grow in love for God and our neighbor, and living out what we understand God is calling us to do.

A great Wesleyan doctrine is about backsliding. Wesley knew we would make mistakes, that we wouldn't always live the way God wants us to, or even live up to our own expectations of ourselves. There would be times in our journey when it seemed as if we were walking up a sand dune. You know, two steps forward, slide one step back. The important thing to remember is that we don't give up when we fail, or falter. Rather, we pick ourselves up, with God's help, ask for and receive God's forgiveness, and go on with the journey again. There will be times when we are discouraged—times when we feel as if God has forgotten us, when we are "heavy" with doubt or grief or despair. But God is present with us in all those times (whether we are aware of God's presence or not). Remember the image of the house? There are times when all is not well with the house—the furnace breaks down, the roof leaks, the sewer backs up. But we don't just throw up our hands and move out (although some days we'd like to!). Rather, we stick it out, make the repairs, keep up the maintenance on the house, improve it in little ways, and find contentment in living there. That's how it is with the Christian life. Sometimes something breaks down. Sometimes we'd like to just throw up our hands and forget the whole thing. A part of "going on to perfection" is learning to live with the down times and still trust in God.

One of the strengths of the Wesleyan movement was that people came together in society and in class meetings. These small groups helped people go on to perfection. They were a source of encouragement in down times and a source of accountability when people strayed. The power of the United Methodist Church today is not always in how many people we can get into worship, but how those people support each other in small groups, Sunday School classes, and so on.

PUT IT ANOTHER WAY

We hear a lot of talk these days about "being born again." The doctrine of the new birth was an important one for John Wesley—he preached on it regularly and expected that Christians would experience a new birth. He didn't expect that we would always be able to date the experience of the new birth, as in "Last Tuesday, when I was working at my desk, trying to reconcile lists of figures, God came into my heart and made me a new person." For some people, that does happen. Unfortunately, we have come to see that type of example as the model for all Christians, when God doesn't always work that way in every person. Some Christians never have that kind of experience, and yet they know that God loves them, that God through Jesus Christ forgives them and welcomes them into the family of God.

Wesley's sermon "The Marks of the New Birth" lists some specific changes God works in our lives. One is that we have a renewed faith because God has given us new life. Another mark of the new birth is hope, the assurance that we have found salvation in Jesus Christ. And the third mark is a new love for God and neighbor. In some ways, this is like sanctification. But it is more honest to say this is the beginning of sanctification, the door by which we enter. Read this sermon in its fullness to get the rich flavor of Wesley's understanding of the new birth.

Or, as Wesley says in another analogy, it's like human birth. We aren't mature adults when we are born. We are born in a very short time (relatively). After that, we grow gradually and slowly until we reach puberty, adolescence, and then physical maturity. We also grow emotionally, we grow in social graces, we grow in knowledge. Just so, Wesley says, we are "born again" in God, but we are still babies in the faith. We need time to grow to Christian maturity, to become more like Christ. This process of maturing is what Wesley refers to as "going on to perfection," "sanctification," or being "holy."

IT'S A WAY OF LIFE

So holiness, for Wesley, is not something that we flout, like a sticker that says, "I gave blood," or "I voted today," or whatever other good deed we have done or honor we have received. Rather, holiness is a way of life. It's the way we go about our daily business trying to be Christians. It's the way we ask, not just "What Would Jesus Do?" but what would Jesus want me to do about my spiritual growth? What would Jesus want me to do about helping with the food kitchen, or with building that house for Habitat for Humanity? What would Jesus want me to do about the way I discipline my children, or make time to tell them stories about the faith? What would Jesus want me to do as his disciple about the way I do my daily work?

QUESTIONS FOR REFLECTION

1. What new insights do you have about perfection, or holiness, in the Christian life?

2. Read or sing "Love Divine, All Loves Excelling" (*The United Methodist Hymnal* #384). How does this hymn connect with the life of perfection, as it is outlined in this chapter?

3. What new practices, or disciplines, would you like to try in your life as you work on holiness?

4. If holiness means, among other things, that God doesn't leave you where you are, where do you feel God nudging you? Where do you need to grow? What challenges do you need to take on?

FOR FURTHER READING

Scott J. Jones, *United Methodist Doctrine: The Extreme Center* (Nashville: Abingdon Press, 2002).

Steve Mansker, *A Perfect Love* (Nashville: Upper Room, 2004).

John Wesley, Sermon # XVIII, "The Marks of the New Birth," and XLV, "The New Birth," from *The Works of John Wesley*, a multi-volume collection of Wesley's sermons, journals, diaries, hymns, and letters.

Charles Yrigoyen, Jr., *John Wesley: Holiness of Heart and Life* (Nashville: Abingdon Press, 1996).

CHAPTER FIVE

Now You've Gone to Meddling

"You can't build a straight wall out of crooked bricks."

"You can build a crooked wall out of straight bricks."

It's so much fun to listen to preachers argue, particularly when they get carried away with their own rhetoric. The first preacher in the argument above was trying to make a point about the primacy of evangelism in the Christian life. He was focused on repentance, salvation, and new birth. He was trying to say that you need all those things if you are going to have a vital faith. The second preacher was in the "social action camp." She was aware that the Christian life is more than evangelism. She was trying to say that you can have all the "saved" Christians you want, but that they have to do something about their faith, to live it out in the social, political, and economic areas, if it's going to be a vital faith.

The truth is, we need evangelism and social action, a warmed heart and dirty hands. John Wesley was clear about that. He wanted the Methodist people to be born again. He also wanted them involved in works that would change society. Wesley referred to those works as works of mercy. Beyond works of mercy (though this is not Wesley's language) are works of justice. Sometimes, it just isn't enough to feed the hungry. We have to ask questions about what's wrong with a society in which people are hungry? Why can't we, as a nation, feed the hungry, provide medical care for the sick, house the homeless, and so on? If the problem is in the systems that deliver those goods, do we need to change the systems? In this chapter, we will explore the concept of "social holiness," looking at it both theologically and spiritually. Then, in the chapters that follow, we'll look at how that holiness found expression in specific areas on English life in the eighteenth century, and how Wesley's example can become a model for United Methodists in the twenty-first century.

WESLEY AND SOCIAL HOLINESS

First, we have to recognize that Wesley was a social, political, and ecclesiastical conservative. His early nurture and the thought-world in which he lived did not give him the freedom to organize active programs of resistance and social change. In spite of that, both his actions and writings lay the groundwork for social action. The General Rules urged the people called Methodists to resist evil and to do good. Those are open-ended statements—there are no limits on resisting evil and doing good. Therefore, when we notice that we are providing food for larger numbers of people each week at the food bank, we can rejoice that we are feeding the hungry. But, sometimes, we need to do more than that. We need to ask, Why are so many more people hungry? What's happening that they cannot earn a living

and feed their families? Is there a fatal flaw in the current economic system that works against these people being able to
make enough money to buy food? Wesley may not have raised
the question in exactly that way, but he did set out to both provide immediate relief and work to bring about social change so
the relief would not be necessary.

Chapters 6-15 provide examples of how this process worked
out in Wesley's life in a wide range of social, economic, and
political arenas, and we'll save the specifics for those chapters.
Here we raise a more basic question. How did Wesley's understanding of sanctification (holiness) provide a theological
foundation for "social holiness," for what we have chosen to
call "works of justice"?

Sanctification, for Wesley, involved the whole person, living
in the reality of a whole world. The idea of the kingdom of God
was not, for him, just something that individuals work toward
in their personal lives. Rather, he was concerned about the
whole of life. Holiness was not just the way one said one's
prayers, or related to God in private ways. Holiness involved
doing good to others, and, sometimes, doing good meant challenging social, political, and economic systems.

Can I be holy if my brother or sister is hungry, or homeless,
or in prison, or sick, or a slave? Can I be holy if I do not do
everything in my power to change the situation in which my
brother or sister finds himself or herself? Sometimes what I do
is the simple act of charity and personal caring; sometimes what
I do must involve challenging the systems that put my brother
or sister in that situation.

While Wesley did not use that language, he lived it out, as
we'll see in the following chapters.

He did set a pattern for a Christian response in the secular
world to bring about justice in the name of Christ.

AND WHAT ABOUT US?

As we begin to think about social holiness in our own lives, we pause to look at some basic documents about faith and life in twenty-first century United Methodism. The first is "The Baptismal Covenant I," the order for baptism and confirmation in our beloved church. At baptism, the questions are asked:

Do you renounce the spiritual forces of wickedness, reject the evil powers of this world, and repent of your sin?

Do you accept the freedom and power God gives you to resist evil, injustice, and oppression in whatever forms they present themselves? (*The United Methodist Hymnal,* p. 34)

The Christian life, for United Methodists, is rooted first in grace and then grows toward social justice and holiness. The questions suggest, first, that there are spiritual powers that we need to reject. Paul called these the "principalities and powers." We tend to refer to them as "isms" and call them by such names as racism, sexism, ageism, and so on. The spiritual powers are those realities

A note on the use of words is important here. Often, when we talk about justice, we mean something more like revenge. We want "justice" done to a murderer, or rapist, for example. Justice, as we use it here, means working toward a more just, or fair, social order. It means working toward an order where each person finds his or her basic needs met, and has the opportunity to improve her or his situation. In the Bible, justice is most often defined as caring for the widow, the orphan and the resident alien. These were the people on the margins of society, people who had no legal rights or protections and most stood in need of the community's help. The Psalms, the prophets, and the wisdom writers all judge the rule of the king, or the success of society, on the basis of how they care for those who are not in a position to care for themselves.

that are more than just the sum of the sins of individuals—they exist above and beyond individual sins. The evil and injustice we're talking about here are sums that are greater than the whole of the parts. They are "spiritual forces of wickedness." Racism, for example, is a reality that is more than just the accumulation of the racial feelings of however many billions of people there are on the earth this week. It is a pervasive evil that infects us, even as it feeds on our own feelings about race. In a life committed to holiness, we battle against these spiritual forces of wickedness. Sometimes that battle involves political and social action.

The questions also proclaim that God gives us the freedom to resist evil and injustice in all its forms. God sets us free to resist racism, economic oppression, dictatorship, attacks on human rights, and/or anything else that denies to any person the opportunity for the fullest possible life. To live a holy life means resisting them in all the ways we can. Some Christians choose to resist by refusing to participate in war, or protesting against war. Others buy stocks in companies and try to change company policies through action at stockholders' meetings. Still others work to influence city councils, state legislatures, or Congress to change laws they perceive to be unjust. A holy life means more than praying, reading the Bible, or attending worship. It even means more than doing good works, caring for the needs of our neighbors. A holy life also works with others to try to bring the political, social, and economic systems of our age into something that resembles the Kingdom of God. And the holy life grows out of the grace of God, as that grace fills our lives and changes us.

The second basic document at which we need to look is the "Social Principles." This document is an attempt on the part of the church to speak to issues in today's world that are larger than the individual, or the individual's attempt to bring about justice in those issues. The Social Principles call upon the whole church, the people of God, to work together to resist evil and oppression in these areas. Individuals obviously have to contribute to this work, but it requires the combined efforts of the whole church to bring about significant and lasting change.

The Social Principles are written/rewritten every four years by the General Conference (the only body that can officially speak for the United Methodist Church). Because they can be rewritten every four years, positions taken by the church may change, in the light of either new knowledge on a subject or new discernment of God's will on the part of the church. Some issues drop out, as situations change. Other issues appear, as new questions arise. The Social Principles are grounded in theological and biblical understandings, and the General Conference attempts to apply those understandings, as faithfully as possible, to specific questions in our world. There are six sections in the Social Principles, each section dealing with an overarching area of concern. They are:

The Natural World, which includes space, energy, science and technology and the environment.

The Nurturing Community includes the family, marriage, divorce, sexuality, abortion, death with dignity, and other topics.

The Social Community deals with racism, the rights of religious minorities, children, youth, the aging, women, persons with disabilities, persons of different sexual orientations; questions of population, alcohol and drugs, medical experimentation, genetic technology, rural life, media violence, the right to health care, and organ transplantation and donation.

The Economic Community deals with property, collective bargaining, work and leisure, consumption, poverty, migrant workers, and gambling.

The Political Community deals with basic freedoms, political responsibility, education, civil obedience and disobedience, criminal justice, military service.

The World Community addresses nations and cultures, national power and responsibility, war and peace, justice and law within a global context.

The Social Principles cover a wide range of topics, many of which come out of Wesley's basic concerns. Some of the statements may surprise you. Did you know, for example, that the Social Principles consider war to be "incompatible with the teachings and example of Christ"? The conclusions the Social Principles draw from that phrase are startling, to say the least, in the light of all the wars in which we find ourselves engaged. That is only one example of how the Social Principles offer guidance of the life of holiness in our world.

Do we have to believe in The Social Principles in order to be United Methodists? No, but since they are official statements of our church, we have to take them seriously. When we disagree, we need to be aware of the reasons for our disagreement in the light of the teachings of our church, and to ask ourselves how our own actions may contribute more to social holiness than does the statement of the church.

QUESTIONS FOR REFLECTION

1. What does the word "justice" mean to you? What does the Bible say about justice? How does Jesus define justice?

2. What does it mean to you to deny the spiritual forces of wickedness, or resist evil and injustice in all their forms? What new insights about holiness (and the consequences of baptism) do you have as a result of reading this chapter?

3. Borrow a copy of The Social Principles from your church and read them carefully. (You will find them in *The Book of*

Discipline or printed in a separate pamphlet. You can also find them on the web by doing a simple search.) Make careful note of where your reading causes you to say, "I didn't know that." Make careful note of where your reading causes you to say, "I need to do something about that." Think of other people in your congregation who would work with you. Pray about next steps in your life.

FOR FURTHER READING

Manfred Marquardt, *John Wesley's Social Ethics* (Nashville: Abingdon Press, 1992).

CHAPTER SIX

Life in Wesley's England

Look at these newspaper headlines:

Jobless Rate Goes Up for Sixth Straight Year

Demonstrations and Riots over Job Loss

Military Veterans Come Home to No Benefits

Changing Economy Threatens to Wipe Out Middle Class

Tax Structure Unfair—but to Whom?

Rebels and Terrorists Attack Troops on Holy Day

Hundreds of Thousands More Slide into Poverty

Health Care System Failing; Thousands Without Adequate Care

Those all sound depressingly familiar, don't they? They come from the headlines we read in the paper every day. Actually, they could come equally well from the United States today and from England in the eighteenth century. Which makes us think again about how anything that John Wesley said in eighteenth century England could possibly be relevant for twenty-first century America. "The more things change, the more they stay the same." We continue to face the same social, economic, and political problems that Wesley faced over 200 years ago. In this chapter, we'll look at some of the issues Wesley faced in his England. Then, in the rest of the book, we'll look at some issues from our day, explore parallels with Wesley's day, see how he responded to the issues, and, finally, identify some ways in which Wesley could be a model for our Christian lives today.

First, the eighteenth century was a century of wars. Sound familiar? During the eighteenth century, Great Britain was involved in

The War of Spanish Succession

The War of the Triple Alliance

The War of the Austrian Succession

King George's War (in North America)

The Scots Rebellion in support of "Bonnie Prince Charlie"

Colonial wars in India that led to British domination there

The "French and Indian War" in North America

The American Revolution, which also led to war with France and Spain

The Anglo-Dutch war

The French Revolution and war with France

The Irish Rebellion under Wolfe Tone.

And there were wars on the European Continent between other powers, each of which threatened to pull in the British. Great Britain became a military state, with an emphasis on manufacturing guns, powder, ships, uniforms, and so on. The demands of both the army and navy for men meant that young men (and many not so young) spent years in military service. When a war ended, they were discharged, with no benefits or help to ease their way back into society. Even worse was the fate of those who were discharged because they were so severely wounded they could no longer serve. They were left to beg or depend on the charity of others. Finally, the demands for manpower were so great that England alone could not fill the ranks of the army and navy. Thousands of German mercenaries were hired to fight in the armies of England. These included those famous "Hessians" who were so thoroughly hated by the American colonists before and during the American Revolution.

At the same time, the Industrial Revolution was beginning to have an effect on the English society and economy. Early in the eighteenth century, we have the invention of the flying shuttle loom, which led to mass production of textiles. Rubber was introduced into England in 1736. In 1742, cotton factories were established in Birmingham and Northampton. These factories would have a powerful effect on English economic and social life, as well as promote the cultivation of cotton in the new world, and increase the dependence on slavery in the American south. In 1758 the ribbing machine, for the manufacture of hose (stockings for both men and women, including the military) was invented. In 1765, both the spinning jenny and an improved steam engine appeared. These were two more steps toward the factory system in England. In 1773, the year of the "Boston Tea Party," the first cast-iron bridge in England was built. John Wesley was fascinated by this bridge and went out of his way on one of his circuits to see the bridge and describe it in his *Journal*. By 1785, England saw the development of the power loom for cloth making. Steam became the major source of power in English factories. This would also increase the demand for coal, and make coal miners a force in the economy. At the end of the century, Eli Whitney (in the United States) developed the cotton gin, another invention that made cotton growing more profitable. Whitney also developed a system of manufacture using interchangeable parts, which would revolutionize the manufacturing process in both England and America. As is so often the case, the first use of interchangeable parts was in the manufacture of firearms.

The military and, particularly, the economic changes in England had a profound impact on the lives of individuals, particularly the poor. At the beginning of the eighteenth century, the number of the poor varied from year to year, and from one part of England to another, depending on the harvest. In good years, there were fewer poor, for more people had enough to eat. There was a strong middle class, made up primarily of skilled workers and craftsmen. They were based in homes, and worked at a trade or craft (pottery making, weaving, carpentry, and so on). This part of the middle class would disappear with the beginning of the Industrial Revolution, as factories made their skills and products obsolete. Shopkeepers, tradesmen, and innkeepers were also a part of the middle class. They were not affected by the Industrial Revolution as much as workers in the crafts, but their income varied depending on social and economic factors far beyond their control.

Already in the early 1700s, the poor were the largest part of the population. The gap between the rich and the poor was steadily growing. All through the century, the numbers of the poor increased. Most of them did not have any schooling or vocational training. Most of them no longer lived in their home communities, but gathered in industrial areas, or in slums at the fringes of the cities. They had no medical care, and the mortality rate among these poor classes was incredibly high. In spite of all this, the population continued to grow, due to an extremely high birthrate. The population growth put an added strain on the economy and made food even scarcer. One of Wesley's continuing concerns was the scarcity of food for the poor, as we will see in chapter 8.

In rural areas, large landowners began to move their tenants off the farms they had worked for years. Because of the high demand for wool by the clothing industry, landowners stopped depending on crops raised by tenant farmers and "enclosed" their lands, to make vast pastures for flocks of sheep. (This consolidation of farms is not unlike what happened in the rural United States during the last half of the twentieth century.) The property owners, often absentee, were the only people who gained from this movement. The dispossessed farm workers drifted away, trying to find some kind of work for which they were qualified. After 1760, the pace of this process stepped up, creating a large pool of unemployed persons. This, in turn, depressed wages in the industrial sector. The invention of the steam engine, spinning jenny, and all the other labor-saving devices increased unemployment. Jobs simply disappeared. Independent craftsmen lost their economic security and fell into dependence on wages. This meant continual insecurity, and, often, total loss of income.

With a large pool of unemployed, the exploitation of workers became common. Women and children worked ten to twelve hour days, seven days a week. Working conditions in most industries were inhumane—what we would now call sweatshops probably would only be a pale imitation of the inhumanity in which workers, particularly miners, slaved. Low wages, lack of food and medical care, brutality by employers, led to anger and desperation on the part of the workers. Local demonstrations sometimes led to violence. The authorities did nothing to improve conditions that led to protests. Instead, they saw any disturbance as an attack on the privileges of the wealthy. The army was often used to intervene, to put down demonstrations (usually violently) and then impose severe punishment on the workers.

These political, economic, and social conditions formed the backdrop against which Wesley launched the Revival and the great concern for the poor that accompanied it.

QUESTIONS FOR REFLECTION

1. What similarities do you see between Wesley's world and our own? What issues are still the same? What issues have disappeared? What new issues have taken their place?

2. As you read your newspaper, or watch the news on television or the web, what issues make you say, "Shouldn't someone do something about that?" Could you be that someone? What other reactions do you have to items in the news? Take note of them, and begin to ask yourself about the connection between those reactions and Wesley's call to a life of holiness.

FOR FURTHER READING

J. Wesley Bready, *England Before and After Wesley: The Evangelical Revival and Social Reform* (London: Hodder and Sthoughton, n.d.).

Henry D. Rack, *Reasonable Enthusiast: John Wesley and the Rise of Methodism* (Philadelphia: Trinity Press International, 1989).

Chapter Seven

If You Can Read This, You're Special!

You're special if you can read this: many adults in the United States cannot read. The National Institute for Literacy says that 20% of adults read at or below the fifth grade level. This is far below the level needed to earn a living wage!

The National Adult Literacy Survey says that 42 million Americans over the age of sixteen cannot read. Some can write their names on Social Security cards and fill in height, weight, and birth date on application forms.

Fifty-five to sixty million are limited to sixth, seventh, and eighth grade reading. They could not figure the cost per ounce of peanut butter in a twenty ounce jar costing $1.99. Not even when they were told they could round the price to an even $2.00!

What is frightening about those numbers is that these are not citizens in some third world country! These are citizens of the United States. What are the implications? Families headed by an adult who cannot read are more likely to be poor. Many of the people represented by those statistics cannot fill out an employment application. Or, think about this: some of those people cannot read and understand directions on prescription bottles. How do they know how to take medication properly?

"I have to teach to the test. I have no choice. My job, the rating of my school, and the school district, depend on it. So I take two weeks out of students actually learning something so they can pass the test. I hate it, and I think it's disastrous for learning, but there's no choice." (A composite based on conversations with some six to eight teachers in different school districts.) The tension here is between accountability and learning.

A major political debate continues around the question of school vouchers. Proponents argue that vouchers give parents the choice of taking their children out of failing schools and putting them in schools that are succeeding. Opponents argue that vouchers will not solve the problems we find in public schools, but only make them worse. The political argument about vouchers dances around the root problems of education, but does not seem to address them directly.

EDUCATION IN WESLEY'S ENGLAND

In the England of the eighteenth century, there was no uniform system of education. There were Latin schools, church schools, schools founded by factory owners, rural landlords, and even individuals. Latin schools were rich in tradition, but often failed to teach very much. The "public" schools were really private schools that were open only to the children of the wealthy. Their curriculum was based on the humanities. Schools operated by dissenters (Quakers, Presbyterians, Baptists, and so on) focused on the natural sciences and languages. In rural areas there were private schools that taught reading, writing, and arithmetic (for a small fee). At least two of Wesley's sisters taught in these schools for a time. Most children, because their parents could not afford to pay for schooling, had no formal instruction at all. Wesley's mother, Susannah, taught her children at home, because there was no school in Epworth. The Wesley children were fortunate that Susannah was a highly educated woman for her day, and that their father, Samuel, was available to teach them languages. So Samuel Jr., John, and Charles were well prepared for prep school and Oxford.

FOUNDING SCHOOLS

Who would have thought that one man's quest for holy living would lead to radical social change in unexpected places? Wesley was able to move England toward a system of basic elementary education for all children because he believed so strongly that all persons are children of God and therefore of equal worth in the world. If all children are of equal worth, why should only some receive the privilege of an education? Should not all children have the right to learn? Are not literacy and numeracy basic human rights? Wesley might not have used that language, but the language does echo his thoughts about education. Education was an important part of Wesley's program of social action.

Wesley began promoting education early in his adult life. While Wesley was on staff at Lincoln College, he and his younger brother, Charles, met with other students at Oxford for prayer, Bible study, and religious conversation. This group would later be known as the "Holy Club." The Holy Club at Oxford helped support teachers for poor children. In Georgia he tried to teach the children of his parish. But it was only after the beginning of the Revival that education took a prominent place in his social agenda.

In 1739, Wesley began building the first school at Kingswood, near Bristol. This was for the coal miners of the area, adults who had had no opportunity for formal schooling. The school came out of a deep religious conviction. Wesley believed that the miners were worthy in God's sight and should have the opportunity to become full human beings, and develop a sense of self-worth. He started other schools for the poor in Bristol, London, and Newcastle-upon-Tyne. The adult students in these schools learned reading, writing, and the Christian faith.

Wesley taught the same basic subjects to children. Children were educated free of charge if their parents could not afford to pay anything for education. Needy children were also given clothing and meals. The money for all these activities came from gifts from the Methodist societies and philanthropic nobles. Wesley turned the money over to administrators, who oversaw the day-to-day operations of the schools.

In 1748, Wesley began the project that was always dear to his heart—the Kingswood School for children. In 1749, there were four Methodist schools in Kingswood. There was a day school for boys, a day school for girls, an orphan school for girls, and the "new House" as Wesley called the 1748 project. Wesley had a clear plan for the schools, based on both his own religious conviction of the need for equal educational opportunities and his criticism of the existing schools and their educational methods. Henry Rack points out that Wesley had four criticisms of the existing schools:

they were mostly near to large towns and therefore near to diversion and corrupting company:

all sorts were admitted;

most of the masters had no more religion than the scholars;

the instruction was poorly planned. Latin and Greek predominated, at the expense of more elementary work. (Rack, p. 355)

Wesley lived in a day when free public education was totally unknown, and his "options" were either inferior private schools or no education at all for the poor. Wesley clearly saw himself as an educational as well as a religious reformer. He planned the Kingswood schools so they would be set apart in the countryside, yet close enough to Bristol to easily obtain supplies. He took only select students, and they boarded. It was important to Wesley that his students stay at school to avoid interference from parents (usually in the form of poor moral examples). The purpose of the school was "forming their minds, through the help of God, to wisdom and holiness, by instilling the principles of true religion, speculative and practical, and training them up in the ancient way, that they might be rational, scriptural Christians." (quoted in Rack, p. 356) Notice that he was concerned with both Scripture and reason. He wanted his students to be grounded in Scripture, but he also wanted them to be critical thinkers. This is an important reminder for our day, when we often separate critical thought and biblical knowledge. Wesley seemed to believe that critical thought would enhance faith, not destroy it.

Wesley's educational theory, if we can call it that, was based on his own childhood and Susannah's practice. He thought it was important to "break the will" of a child, who would then be more willing to learn. He had no use for what we would call "child-centered education." He said, "Religion should be instilled as soon as possible because Scripture, reason and experience show that the corruption of human nature should be curbed from the first . . . . This should be done by 'mildness' where this is possible, but by 'kind severity' where it is not. The purpose is to move children from the love of the world to love of God." (Rack, p. 354)

The students at Kingswood followed a strict regimen, based on Wesley's own practice, though he did allow children more time for sleeping. The curriculum included reading, writing, arithmetic, English, French, Latin, Greek, Hebrew, history, geography, chronology, rhetoric, logic, ethics, geometry, algebra, physics, and music. In practice, French, algebra, and music were neglected. In fact, Wesley had a fairly low opinion of French as a language. Note these courses were for children ages six to twelve! Wesley also wanted to found a four-year academy to teach the classics, modern science, history, and literature. This dream did not come true until the 1760s, when Oxford blocked Methodist students from attending there. Oxford' action resulted in an academy that Wesley suggested gave young adults a better education than Oxford could. One suspects this statement came from some deep hurt Wesley felt because the college he loved rejected the students he loved.

EDUCATING THE PREACHERS

Wesley was always concerned for educating his preachers. Some of them, of course, were ordained, and had degrees from Oxford or Cambridge. But the lay preachers had little or no formal schooling in theology and the arts. So, beginning in 1745, Wesley began working on a list of books for the preachers to read. These included works in natural philosophy(science), history, poetry, divinity, and the classics. Wesley wanted to be, in his words, *homo unius libri,* a "man of one book," meaning the Bible. It is clear, however, that his intellectual interests ranged widely and he wanted his preachers to engage in dialogue between the Bible and other books. It seems plausible that Wesley wanted his preachers to be in touch with the best learning of his day so that they could, in turn, witness to the gospel to those who were specialists in particular fields.

One of Wesley's great educational projects was *The Christian Library,* a series of books for his preachers (primarily) to read. These were carefully edited and condensed religious classics. Wesley was interested in a wide range of reading and thought but he also didn't want his preachers to be "infected" by what he felt were false doctrines. So the Bible remained the foundation for theological education and Christian spiritual formation.

EDUCATION AND THE SOCIETIES

Wesley did not do all this education work alone. He regularly preached and taught on the education of children. He checked on the schools he started, to be sure that the instructors were being faithful to their tasks. He talked with the children, taught them the faith, told them stories. He taught, from time to time, in the schools, he wrote school books(!), outlined the basic plan of instruction, talked to parents about raising their children as Christians. All this, in addition to everything else he was doing!

In addition, he required the preachers to preach on topics about child-rearing and the importance of education. They were to report to the congregations on the work of the schools and to take offerings for the schools.

Methodist societies emphasized holiness of heart and reading gave people a way to better seek such holiness. The audience was primarily people who had not attended school and who may have learned to read as adults. Wesley felt that reading Christians were more secure in their faith. A systematic program of reading encouraged Methodists to think about basic issues of life and faith. Wesley wanted them to read and to talk to each other about what they read. The reading programs developed by United Methodist Women today are an echo of Wesley's concern for educated Christians, although most United Methodist Women are more than able to read. Wesley felt that uneducated people should not be excluded from the joys and benefits of reading. He wanted them to learn to read; he wanted them to read the materials he provided for them.

It is not an exaggeration to say that the duty towards education that Wesley instilled in the societies was a key to changing the educational system in England.

Even today, when United Methodist ministers become full members of the annual conference, they are asked, among other historic questions, "Will you diligently instruct the children in every place?" (*Book of Discipline*, ¶ 327) This is one of the questions Wesley asked his preachers, and his concern for educating children continues to our day.

THE SUNDAY SCHOOL

The first Methodist Sunday School was established in 1769 by Hannah Ball, in High Wycombe. It was intended primarily for those children who had to work the other six days of the week. Since their parents often worked seven days a week, having a Sunday School was a service to the family, since it kept young children from being unsupervised that day. The schools taught reading, writing, and the most important parts of the catechism. In some places, the children also learned arithmetic. Their basic text was the Bible, as it was in most schools of the day. Though Wesley was not a leader in starting Sunday Schools, he approved of them and promoted them whenever possible. Out of his deep social concern, he saw the Sunday School as one more way to help the poor.

LITERATURE AND PRINTING

Educating the poor was left entirely to voluntary organizations, and the need was greater than they could meet. Wesley began to provide inexpensive literature for the schools and also for individual reading. The Society for the Promotion of Christian Knowledge was his model and ally in this part of his ministry. He saw his writing as a way to spread the Gospel, and to deepen the faith of Christians. In addition, writing was a way of carrying on theological discussions with his opponents. Some of his most famous "letters" were really tracts, designed for theological debate with Roman Catholics, Calvinists, and others. When these tracts were printed and circulated, they became another tool for educating both the people called Methodists, and the wider public.

Wesley used the most modern technology of his day to provide the poor with books. Though this is not the same as using power point in worship, Wesley's aim was to offer salvation and educate the poor, and help them grow in the faith, totally outside the worship experience. He wrote on a wide variety of subjects—religion, practical issues, biography, travel, poetry, and philosophy. He printed his *Journal,* and it went through many editions in his lifetime. His *Sermons* also went through many editions. He charged only minimal prices for his writings, because he wanted the poor to be able to afford them. If anyone could not pay, the books were to be given away.

One of his books, called *Primitive Physic,* was a major best seller in England and in America. It was a collection of remedies for various illnesses. The primary purpose of *Primitive Physic* was Wesley's wholistic concern for people's needs, particularly salvation. He believed that God cared for bodies as well as souls. Some of his suggested remedies were serious helps for illnesses, others were folk remedies that we would find only amusing. In 1778, Wesley began the *Arminian Magazine* as a response to the Calvinist magazines circulating in England.

WHAT CAN WE LEARN FROM WESLEY?

Wesley read everything he could get his hands on, and applied most of his reading to his preaching and writing. That suggests that we also need to be well-read, particularly on key controversial topics. If we are, as Christians, going to weigh in on moral arguments about such topics as cloning, stem-cell research, abortion, homosexuality, evolution, and a host of other topics, then we need to know as much about those topics as possible. It's hard to discuss the ethics of stem-cell research, for example, if we don't know what the science, the possibilities and the negatives of stem-cell research are. It is not enough simply to say that this research (or any other) is wrong, just because we feel that way in our "gut." If we want to have any influence in the public arena, we need to be informed.

Second, in our language, learning is more important than teaching for the results of the test. Wesley wanted his followers to master knowledge, to know how to apply knowledge to life, and to think critically.

Third, Wesley was committed to using the most modern technology to promote education. In his day, that technology was the printing press. What is the most effective technology we can use today to promote learning? That seems obvious, correct? The most effective technology clearly is the computer and the Internet. But, (see the next paragraph) the most effective technology is out of the reach of the poor, and the gap in educational opportunity and quality grows wider. How do we, as the people of God, make it possible for the poor to have access to the most modern technology available, so that they don't fall farther behind?

Fourth, Wesley was committed to education for the poor. His commitment ranged from starting free schools for the poor to providing reading materials. Given the rate of illiteracy in the United States, and the connection between illiteracy and poverty, what steps should United Methodists be taking to minister in practical ways to this segment of our population?

Finally, Wesley started a grand tradition for Methodists. We call it "you don't have to check your brains at the door." We United Methodists are invited to think for ourselves, to raise questions, and debate answers. We don't have to blindly follow anyone in a leadership position, but are set free by God (as

Wesley would say) to learn and think for ourselves. We certainly expect those in authority over us to challenge us, stir us to learning and action, and stretch our minds. But we are free to think for ourselves.

QUESTIONS FOR REFLECTION

1. Why did Wesley say that literacy and a broad-based education were important for Christians? What was his theological rationale for literacy? His practical rationale? Would you agree or disagree with him? Why?

2. What does it mean to you that "We Methodists don't have to check our brains at the door" when we come to worship?

3. How is our commitment to ministry with the poor linked to literacy? If literacy can help people escape from poverty, what is your congregation doing to help in this process? What literacy programs are working in your community? How could your congregation support those programs as part of a wider ministry?

CHAPTER EIGHT

The Economic Question

"It's the economy" has been a catch phrase in American politics since the election cycle of 1992, when Bill Clinton rode it to victory over George II.W. Bush. "Are you better off now than you were four years ago?" was another famous campaign question, one that continues to surface after every economic downturn. On the one hand, those slogans remind us that we focus better on bread-and-butter issues than on international questions. On the other hand, they also remind us that most of our focus on economic issues is on ourselves and how the economy affects us.

"The one who dies with the most toys, wins!" (Bumper sticker often seen around the nation)

As this book is being written, economic issues struggle with news of terrorism and war to capture our attention. We learned recently that the number of persons living in poverty in the United States increased significantly over the past year. A large minority of those persons in poverty were children and seniors, and neither group was able to do much to directly change their economic condition. Economic "reforms" were threatening to eliminate overtime pay for many persons in the work force—a move that would push more families closer to poverty. Jobs were being shipped overseas and CEOs were rewarded for that. Workers were losing their pension funds while executives pillaged corporations. The economic news in the United States has not been good. We also wonder what the costs of war will do to the economy, and what another September-11-type attack might do.

What does that mean for real people? For some, it's all bad news. A recent study showed that one in every five jobs in the United States pays less that a poverty level wage for a family of four. That's thirty-nine million Americans, including twenty million children. These working families struggle to meet basic needs, such as housing, groceries, and childcare. The poverty level income in 2002 was identified as $18, 244. (AOL News, October 11, 2004)

IT'S THE RELIGIOUS QUESTION!

For John Wesley, all economic problems were ethical problems. And, therefore, they were religious questions. Wesley believed that religion was not confined to Sunday morning, but related to all of life. In his day, as in ours, the problems of making a living took up most of a person's waking hours. Therefore, he argued, the whole area of economics is the most obvious place for Christians to work at cultivating holy living. If we don't develop character and virtue in the economic world, he argued, where will we? If Christian character and holiness of life do not influence economic matters, what is the point of preaching Christ? The Bible itself is full of words relating to economic matters. As only one example, see James 2:1-7 and 4:13–5:6. What did that mean for Wesley, in practical terms?

Wesley had a life-long interest in the bread-and-butter issues of life. It may well be that being raised in poverty, and being teased at Charterhouse (the prep school he attended on a scholarship reserved for the poor) about his poverty had a great deal to do with that interest. The people among whom he served were, by and large, engaged in a grim, day-to-day, struggle for food and shelter. They were among the poorest of the poor. Some entries in Wesley's Journal illustrate his concern for the conditions of the poor.

> In the afternoon I visited many of the sick; but such scenes, who could be unmoved? There are none such to be found in a Pagan country. If any of the Indians in Georgia were sick…those that were near him gave him whatever he wanted. O who will convert the English into honest Heathens!
>
> On *Friday* and *Saturday* I visited as many more as I could. I found some in their cells under ground; others in their garrets, half-starved both with cold and hunger, added to weakness and pain. But I found not one of them unemployed, who was able to crawl about the room. So wickedly, devilishly false is that common objection, "They are poor, only because they are idle." If you saw those things with your own eyes, could you lay out money in ornaments or superfluities? (February 8–10, 1753, Journals, Vol. II, pages 279-280)

Wesley reacted to poverty in two ways. On one level, he did everything he could to care for the poor. On another level, he attacked the economic injustices of his day and proposed specific remedies to those injustices. And he did this on the ground of Christian ethics and the importance of living out one's faith in every area of life.

We saw, in chapter 2, how "doing good works" was a key part of his prescription for the Christian life. Beginning at Oxford, he and his followers provided food, clothing, education, medicine, and social services for the poor whenever and wherever they could. One of the guidelines for the bands and societies was that each member would bring a penny every week (remember, these were very poor people, and a penny went a lot farther in those days) to be used to care for the poor. When he was in his late eighties, Wesley spent one Christmas Eve wading in ankle-deep icy slush from door to door, begging for money to help the poor.

But on a deeper level, Wesley looked at poverty and other economic questions through the lens of God's concern for the poor and applied Christian ethics to larger questions of economic policy. First, he laid out rules for using money, in spite of the fact that most Methodists didn't have any! He did this for two reasons: 1) most Christians didn't know how to deal with money, and no one offered them any instructions, and 2) the use of money (for good or ill) had a profound effect for both the Christian and his neighbor. Even with all the "how-to" books on using money to make money that we have at our disposal, and all the financial planners whom we consult for advice, Wesley's three simple rules are still among the best advice we could find.

Those "rules" are found in his famous sermon, *On The Use of Money*. They are, indeed, simple rules, and can be summarized in three sentences:

> Earn all you can
>
> Save all you can, so
>
> You can give all you can.

To fully appreciate the power of those rules, we need to look at them in more detail. First, Wesley urged the Methodists (and others) to "earn all you can." The limit on this rule was that one had to be honest in one's dealings with others. People in business were to give honest weight, not overcharge, take only a fair profit and not take advantage of their neighbors, and so on. Wesley was a political and economic conservative, who believed in liberty, but he always wanted to restrict liberty with honesty and openness. Within the boundaries of honesty and concern for others, one was free to earn all one could in honorable occupations. The choice of an occupation or vocation, for Wesley, had little to do with one's abilities or wishes, but with 1) is the occupation an honorable one? and 2) is it an occupation that will allow us to serve God and our neighbor? He would have had little patience with the person overheard saying, "I don't care what I do when I get out of school. I just want to be a millionaire!"

The best way to improve the living conditions of the poor was for them to earn all they could, and then to save all they could, after they had taken care of the necessities of food, clothing, and shelter. One needed to be thrifty, and to be diligent about saving. Don't buy anything you don't really need. Put the money into savings accounts instead. In our day, the rate of individual savings is at an all-time low. At the same time, individual debt is at an all-time high. Much of the debt is in home mortgages, but an incredibly significant amount is in credit card debt. Wesley might say to us, is it really necessary that you buy a $50,000 automobile, when you can get one that works just as well for $20,000 or less? Do you really need all the clothes and/or shoes you have in your closet? What if you didn't spend that money, but put it in savings? What difference would that make for your life?

To earn all we can, and to save all we can were not rules about accumulating money for its own sake. Wesley's economic ethics began with the assumption that money, in and of itself, was neither good nor evil. It could become an evil when individuals and corporations (yes, they existed in Wesley's day, too) focused on the accumulation of wealth at the expense of others. When wealth became an end in itself, rather than a means to a greater end, it became an evil. And money did offer the possibilities for effective social help, making it possible for those with money to care for those without it. So, for Wesley, whether or not money was a good or evil depended on how people used it.

To earn all we can, and to save all we can, were means to a greater end for Wesley. That end was found in the third rule, to give all you can. For Wesley, there was a clear boundary between what was necessary for life, and the accumulation of wealth. We express something of the same idea today when we talk about the difference between "needs" and "wants." We also recognize that today's "want" becomes tomorrow's "need;" that is, that we discover our needs tend to grow as we have more disposable wealth. Wesley argued that, once we had met the basic necessities of food, clothing, and shelter, we began to develop an excess of wealth. That excess was to be given to meet the needs of others. He based this argument on an understanding of Christian stewardship. The true owner of all things is God, and whatever property or wealth we have is given to us by God to manage. God teaches us, Wesley argued, that stewardship means giving whatever excess we have beyond the basic necessities of life to help others in need. To give to others was an act of obedience to the commandment to love our neighbor, and to love God in our neighbor. Wesley argued that we will have to account to God for the way we use our wealth. What is the record of our stewardship? Will we be able to say that we have been faithful stewards of God's gifts? That does not mean that Wesley wanted his followers to own all things in common. He believed in the right of private property. He simply emphasized that the property is a gift from God and we need to use it wisely, in ways that please God. Private property, then, was not an absolute right, but a relative one, based on God's ownership of all things, and the call to stewardship.

So what about the wealthy? If we are well-off economically, perhaps even above that magic line of persons making over $200,000 a year, are we condemned? No. Wesley didn't want rich people to give up their possessions. Money can be used for commercial and industrial development. That kind of investment can benefit society as well as the individual. Wesley believed, however, that money for its own sake could lead to both personal and communal pain. The rich, he said, have a special call from God to help others, to use their wealth for the benefit of the poor, and the physical and spiritual welfare of others. When money became an end in itself, then gaining wealth led to social injustice. So, Wesley wanted the wealthy to follow the same simple rules he set up for his poorer followers—earn all you can, save all you can, so you can give all you can.

SOCIETY AND ECONOMIC RESPONSIBILITY

We argue, in our day, about the role of society and government in economic issues. On the one hand, some argue that the poor are poor only because they don't want to work. Against that, there are some stark realities. First, many of the poor are children, who are forbidden to work by law. Second, many of the poor are elderly, who are not physically able to work, even if they could find employment. Third, many of the poor are working—some of them at two or three jobs, just to make ends meet. In a just society, would we have both homeless people and million-dollar homes within the same metropolitan area? On the other hand, most of the suggestions put forward for building a more equitable economic system are either unworkable or incredibly expensive. So is there anything we can learn from John Wesley about how we can work on basic economic structures to make a difference to the poor?

Wesley lived in a time when there were no statistics of the kind that we take for granted today. What he said about England's economy was based on what he saw. However, since he traveled all over the kingdom and worked with so many different groups of people, what he saw qualified him as much as anyone else to make judgments about the economy. What did he see? What did he say? First, he said that poverty was not a failure to work on the part of the poor. There were flaws in the economic system that made it impossible for them to earn a living. We saw, in Chapter 6, that the enclosure of land, and the drying up of the middle class of craftsmen caused a great deal of poverty. The development of machines and mass manufacturing put many others out of work. Nor, Wesley said (to slip into theology for a minute), were people poor because God had "predestined" them to be poor. All his life, Wesley argued against what he perceived as the ungodly statement that God elected some persons to be wealthy and others to be poor, and their economic status was a reflection of their status in God's eyes. Against that Calvinist position, Wesley put forward the essential worth of every person in God's eyes, and the call of God to love all our neighbors, but particularly the poor.

When Wesley looked at the question of poverty in England, he outlined the causes of poverty, denounced those who were guilty of creating and perpetuating a system that put people into poverty, exhorted the poor to work diligently, and worked to influence the wealthy and powerful to take responsibility for eliminating social evils.

In his *Thoughts on the Present Scarcity of Provisions*, Wesley lists the causes of starvation:

> Unemployment
>
> Scarcity and high prices of food
>
> Squandering grain for use in breweries and for the horses of the wealthy
>
> The monopolies on goods
>
> The elimination of small-holder farms (what we could call the traditional family farm)
>
> Rising rents
>
> High taxes as a result of public debt. (Marquardt, p. 44)

Part of his analysis was naïve, of course, just as our statistics-based modern analysis is often naïve. But he hit on some basic issues, both for his day and for ours. Obviously, people are going to be hungry if they can't find work, so the question of unemployment is always crucial. Jobs continue to be a major issue in political campaigns, and the suggestions for increasing employment range from the practical to the incredible. Wesley also saw that public debt was a major contributor to hunger and poverty. We're all familiar with the arguments about the national debt in our society, and what we should do to reduce the debt. There is the political suicide involved in suggesting we raise taxes and/or cut services in order to manage the debt. Then there is the less tangible, but no less frightening, awareness that doing nothing means we leave the debt to our children and grandchildren. The latter means that we continue to enjoy our own comfort at the cost of putting a burden of debt on the shoulders of future generations, thereby cutting back on their economic security. There are, probably, no easy answers, but the question is one that has to be faced eventually.

Those are only two examples of parallels between Wesley's analysis of his own day, and the realities of our day. What to do about them? Wesley believed in liberty, but he was also willing to support legal restrictions on the economy, and even to impose prohibitions on economic development. For example, he argued, on both economic and biblical grounds, that no farm should be larger than £100 a year in income. This would have had the effect of abolishing the great estates, which were the center of political power and influence. He argued that stewardship of the land meant to provide wholesome food at cheap prices, for *all* people. He believed that the great estates decreased the amount of grain, a point that was probably correct, since many productive fields were taken over for sheep pasture, a move that enriched those in the cloth trade.

Wesley was perfectly willing to prohibit the manufacture

and sale of liquor, both because of the consequences of alcohol abuse, and because so much grain was involved in the manufacture, grain that was not available to make bread for the poor, which resulted in higher bread prices. He was against conspicuous consumption, and would have taxed the wealthy for the sake of the poor. He proposed a tax of £5 on every "gentleman's horse". He also recommended abolishing what he called "useless pensions," especially those given to governors of forts and castles which had long since ceased to be of any military value. Now, note that "pensions" meant something entirely different in Wesley's day from what they mean in ours. In his day, it was a subsidy to a wealthy person for, essentially, doing nothing. In our day, a pension is something we earn while we work, so can we can enjoy the necessities when we can no longer work.

Wesley also believed that the king should use his power of taxation to redistribute wealth more equitably, and to provide food and employment for the people. To lower food prices, for example, would increase demand for other goods, which would both improve the economy and produce more jobs. To achieve this end, Wesley felt, the government should intervene and take whatever steps were necessary to ensure lower food prices. He also called for ending the indirect taxes that hit hardest on the poor. This last argument is echoed today in concerns about sales taxes on food and medicine, for example.

When Wesley talked about loving our neighbor, particularly our poor neighbor, he meant far more than stocking food pantries or adopting a family at Christmas time. He believed in those acts of charity, obviously, but his concern went far deeper. He was interested in the economic responsibility of individual Christians to use their wealth as a means to a greater end of helping the poor. He was also interested in Christians coming together to work to change the underlying economic and political structure of society, so that the poor could have a better life.

QUESTIONS FOR REFLECTION

1. Whenever we talk about money, of course, we hit very close to home. What did you read in this chapter that made you angry or upset? Can you identify why you felt this way?

2. What parallels do you see between economic systems in Wesley's day, and in ours? If there are parallels in the systems, and in the results they cause, would some of Wesley's prescriptions for the economy work for us as well?

3. Wesley's famous "three points"—earn all you can, save all you can, so you can give all you can—are a call to a way of life. In a sense, they are about "holiness in economics." If you were to adopt those three points as a guide for your life, what might you have to change? What attitudes would you have to change?

4. Sing or read "Thou Hidden Source of Calm Repose" (*The United Methodist Hymnal*, #153) How do you connect this hymn with Wesley's concern for the poor?

FOR FURTHER READING

Manfred Marquardt, *John Wesley's Social Ethics* (Nashville: Abingdon Press, 1992).

John Wesley, Sermon 51, "The Good Steward"

CHAPTER NINE

Prisons and Prison Reform

"Prison Brings 250 New Jobs to Rural Community." In rural America, one of the great sources of new jobs is prison construction. There are construction jobs from building the prison, and jobs for guards, food service workers, clerical workers, and so on. In fact, far from the NIMBY (not in my back yard) attitude about so many things, rural communities lobby hard to have new prisons built in their area. Prisons, in the United States, are a big business. In spite of the clamor for prisons in rural areas, however, there are still questions about how much of an economic benefit they bring.

"Judges Concerned About Sentencing Requirements." An increasing concern among judges in the United States is the series of mandatory sentencing laws. The issue is that mandatory sentencing requires minimum sentences for a variety of crimes. Many judges feel there should be more freedom to discriminate between first time and repeat offenders, for example.

More and more churches find themselves in some kind of prison ministry, either directly to prisoners, a Bible study or worship service, ministering to families of prison inmates, and so on.

THE LEGAL SYSTEM IN WESLEY'S ENGLAND

One of the legal reforms following the Glorious Revolution of 1688 was that judges were given immunity from attempts to remove them from office. This gave them greater independence and helped the average citizen feel more secure about his or her treatment under the law. This idea of an independent judiciary was built into the Constitution of the United States, and federal judges are appointed for life, rather than re-elected. Some of the states also have independent judiciaries, though in many cases, judges stand for re-election. In recent years, this whole system has come under attack because judges have upheld federal and state constitutions in ways that are unpopular with politicians and special interest groups. In both twenty-first century America and eighteenth century England, however, the commitment to an independent judiciary is a protection for the ordinary citizen.

Another part of the legal system common to both eras is the idea of mandatory sentences. In the United States, this has often applied to drug-related offenses; in Wesley's England, the law was harsher. In the eighteenth century, there were over 200 crimes punishable by death, ranging from shooting a rabbit to murder, from cutting a young tree or stealing five shillings to insurrection. Those were mandatory sentences, and their very existence lessened the security of individuals and undermined respect for the law. People were hanged for what today would be misdemeanors at best, or not even chargeable offenses. Given the economic realities of the day, people were driven to steal bread to feed their families. If they were caught, they could be hanged.

And—does this make sense?—persons who could not pay their debts were thrown into prison and kept there until they could pay their debts. Wesley knew something about this part of the law, since many of the colonists in Georgia were freed from debtors' prison on condition that they migrate to the New World. In fact, his father had once been sent to prison for debt. Susannah had offered to sell her wedding ring to pay for the debt, but Samuel refused. One of the wealthy nobles with whom Samuel was acquainted later paid the debt to set Samuel free. As the century wore on, and England's wars became a world war, debtors and petty criminals were allowed to join the army or navy, rather than be sent to prison. This may not have been a better fate! However, as late as the Napoleonic Wars, debtors were being shipped to Botany Bay, in Australia. There were some serious problems with the legal system in eighteenth century England.

CONDITIONS IN THE PRISONS

Prison conditions were themselves criminal. The administration of the prisons was often contracted out to private individuals. These private administrators made money by extorting it from the prisoners, as well as from the fees paid by the government. The administrators sold alcohol and drugs, allowed prostitution, and often charged large sums for decent food, blankets, and other necessities. A common practice was displaying famous prisoners in a cage or some other contrivance, where the crowds were charged admission to see him or her. Inmates who could not pay the charges were often tortured or left to starve. Men, women, and children were often crowded together in the same large rooms. For many, the only hope of ever getting out of prison came when the prisons were so over-crowded some were released to make room for new prisoners coming in. Hygiene in the prisons was terrible, and the prisons were breeding grounds for infectious diseases.

WESLEY AND THE PRISONS

Wesley and other members of the Holy Club at Oxford visited the prisons in that city regularly and brought spiritual comfort, food, and even education to the prisoners. Wesley once ministered to a convict on the way to the gallows and was amazed that the prisoner received salvation (the amazement came because Wesley himself did not feel he had experienced salvation, and thus didn't see how he could lead anyone else to it.)

Ministry to the poor included ministry to those in prison. From the spring of 1739, John Wesley was conducting services in the London and Bristol prisons. This was while the Revival was in its opening stages, and he was incredibly busy with preaching, organizing classes, and trying to bring some sense of common direction to the movement. He met with prisoners, particularly those on death row, and ministered to their spiritual needs. This met with resistance from the authorities. The sheriffs at Newgate in Bristol restricted his ministry to one service a week, instead of daily. Other authorities refused to let him meet with prisoners condemned to death, even when the prisoners asked for it. Wesley's preaching to prisoners focused on God's love to all humanity, even to those abandoned by society.

Other Methodists followed his example. By 1743, visiting prisoners was a part of the rules of the societies. What happened when Methodists became aware of the plight of prisoners? The same thing that happens whenever and wherever Methodists become aware of human need. They began to provide humanitarian assistance to the prisoners. In later years, as we shall see, their awareness of prison conditions made them strong supporters of prison reform.

For Wesley and his followers, loving one's neighbor and doing good to those in need led almost automatically to prison ministries. This included ministry to the many prisoners of war held in England. Remember this was a century of war, and prisoners were shipped to England from overseas and incarcerated there, often without any of the basic necessities. Methodists collected money to buy these prisoners food, clothing, and bedding.

Wesley publicly wrote about the conditions in all prisons, and suggested steps that could be taken to improve those conditions. This led to serious reform in some places. In Bristol, for example, the entire prison was cleaned (not a small matter!), drunkenness and prostitution were stopped, and Sunday services became a regular part of prison life.

The Methodists also provided opportunities for inmates to work. Remember that many were in prison for debt and were caught on the horns of a dilemma. They could not be released until their debts were paid. But as long as they were in prison, they had no way of making any money to pay off their debts. Wesley arranged for them to get materials for credit, which they used to learn a trade and to earn money to repay both the loan and the debts they owed. This not only got them out of prison, it gave them a trade by which to earn a living once they were free.

MORE THAN "DOING GOOD"

The commitment to prison ministry did not lead immediately to reform, but it did make large numbers of people aware of the needs of prisoners. First, the Methodists set to work to love their neighbor by easing the harshness of prison conditions. Later, because of their awareness and experience, they were willing to support the efforts of those who tried to reform the prison system. This is an interesting model for our time, as well. When good people become aware of human need and minister to that need (whether it is to prisoners, to the poor, to migrant workers, or the homeless) their own lives are changed. Visiting and serving prisoners and the poor is one avenue of grace by which we grow in love for God and neighbor. (See Matthew 25:31-46.)They become more sensitive because they know persons by name who are part of what had previously been an amorphous group. This sensitivity leads us to provide both material help and relationships to these individuals. In turn, we begin to ask questions about why it is necessary that people have to live in those conditions. This prepares the ground for reform, and provides a solid base of support for reform when the time is right.

Wesley himself publicly protested in print about the abuses of the prison system. His protests, in addition to the new awareness of the Methodists about the prisons, helped pave the way for the systematic reform of prisons led by John Howard and others. Wesley protested, both in his own publications and in the newspapers, against:

the appalling conditions of the prisons,

the effect of a prison stay on moral behavior (prisons were a school for crime),

the long judicial proceedings,

the unequal treatment of poor and rich, and

the inhumane treatment of prisoners of war.

Wesley had solid biblical and theological arguments behind his protests, but he went beyond them to point out practical social consequences of the system. This encouraged those who were not moved by religious arguments to join in the move for reform. Anyone who wanted to help was welcome. What Wesley did not do was attack Parliament or the King's ministers, who were ultimately responsible for the prisons. He was too much a conservative for that. His efforts, however, did ultimately lead to reform.

So What Have We Learned?

What have we learned from Wesley about prison ministries and prison reform that we can apply to our own day? The key is actually visiting the prisons and knowing prisoners as people. Christians in our day, as in Wesley's, are called to go where Christ may be found. Jesus said, ". . . for I was hungry and you gave me food. I was thirsty and you gave me something to drink . . . I was in prison and you visited me." (Matt 25:35-36)

Second, we become aware of the needs of prisoners (at whatever level) and respond to those needs. Wesley would remind us that we respond to what prisoners identify as needs and not what we think those needs should be.

Third, ministry to the families of prisoners is important.

Finally, we may become aware of problems that cannot be addressed simply by ministering to individuals. When that happens, we follow Wesley's example of publicly talking about those problems, and calling for changes in the prison system that will lead to reform.

Questions for Reflection

1. Sing or read "Spirit of Faith, Come Down" (*The United Methodist Hymnal* #332) or "Come, Sinners, to the Gospel Feast" (*The United Methodist Hymnal* #339). How do these words relate to our lives and to prison ministries?

CHAPTER TEN

I Was Sick

Health care is perhaps the hot-button issue in our society today. The cost of health care is sky rocketing at a rate five times the rate of inflation. Millions of people in the United States are without health insurance, many of them children. At the beginning of the twenty-first century, 39.2 million persons in the United States under the age of sixty-five were without health insurance. That was one in six of every person not on Medicare. There were 4.3 million children (under the age of eighteen) with no health insurance overage, or nearly one in nine. (National Center for Health Statistics). At the time this book was written, the numbers were even higher, with some estimates as high as 45 million without health insurance. When those people need medical care, they often wind up going to hospital emergency rooms, which is the most expensive medical care they can get. Many persons, particularly senior citizens, have to make choices among food, rent, and prescriptions, because they can't afford them all. There is a battle royal (as of this writing) between the Food and Drug Administration, the Justice Department, and major drug manufacturers on the one hand, and states, individuals, and citizens' groups on the other, about importing prescription drugs from Canada again. A debate is raging over the loss of doctors in many areas because of the high costs of malpractice insurance. Health care in the United States, in spite of all the vast resources at our disposal, is not in a "healthy" situation.

THE MORE THINGS CHANGE . . .

The state of health care in the eighteenth century was low indeed. There was no understanding of the causes of disease. Viruses and bacteria were unheard of. Vaccinations for smallpox appeared before the end of the century, but beyond that, preventive health care was also unheard of. Poor sanitation, poor diet, and general lack of personal hygiene contributed to the spread of disease. The widespread use of poor quality beverage alcohol also weakened resistance to disease. Surgery was crude, limited primarily to amputations, and done without anesthesia. The only anesthesia available to the military, for example, was to give a wounded man as much rum as he could drink, hoping he would get drunk enough to pass out and escape some of the pain involved in amputation. People died in agony with ruptured appendixes, kidney stones, and other such afflictions that are treated routinely today. The poor were particularly vulnerable to waves of diseases such as measles, typhoid, diptheria, dysentery, and so on. They were often not able to get medicine or to see a decent doctor.

BUT IS THAT A RELIGIOUS QUESTION?

John Wesley was always as concerned about the health of the people as he was about their salvation because he believed God cares for the whole person. He was concerned for the whole person—body, mind, and spirit. This concern for health was an expression of the love for neighbor commanded by Christ, and he lived it out all his life. For Wesley, physical health was, indeed, a religious question. Concern for health was a part of holy living. For individuals, simple matters such as hygiene, exercise, and proper diet, were expressions of one's commitment to holy living. For the church, holiness included caring for the sick, even as Jesus said in Matthew 25:36. The Methodists' ministry to the poor included regular visits to the sick, which included providing food, some medicine, and caring concern. This was not enough, however, to deal with the root of the health-care problems. We should remember that language such as "health care" is our term, and not a common part of the eighteenth century vocabulary. The reality certainly was there; the language was different.

In December of 1746 Wesley told the society he intended to establish a clinic for the poor. He began to dispense medicine and treat simple illness himself. Was he qualified to do this? He was certainly not a physician, though he had attended medical lectures before going to Georgia (in case there were no doctors there). He did get the advice of both a physician and a pharmacist and referred serious cases to medical specialists. Within a few months, he had helped some 300 people, all of them without payment.

Wesley could not continue that kind of work for very long without being overwhelmed. Fortunately, his example sparked free medical clinics both within and beyond the Methodist societies.

TWO LEVELS OF HEALTH AND HEALING

Good health and medical care were religious issues for Wesley. So much so, that he often resorted to prayer as an instrument of healing. We tend to look on prayer for healing as a last resort, as in, "There is nothing left to do but pray." Wesley would have said we begin with prayer and then apply medical remedies. Medical authorities today are beginning to recognize what Wesley knew almost three centuries ago—there is a connection between prayer and health. Doctors do not deal only with a symptom or a disease. They deal with a whole person, and that person's emotional and spiritual health has a direct connection to her or his physical health.

So Wesley's healing ministry was intimately connected with his concern for souls (clearly a religious issue!). In his Journal, he records many instances of healing in answer to prayer. In some cases, he learned that an individual's concern for her or his sin had led to either emotional or physical breakdowns. In these cases, medical intervention was not enough. The wounded spirit had to be healed before the body could be healed. So an important part of Wesley's approach to health was pastoral care. He listened carefully to what people had to say about their spiritual health, or lack of it, and worked with them to seek forgiveness and healing from God. In this, he was following the example of Jesus, who often forgave sins before attempting a physical healing.

On another level, Wesley was concerned for basic rules of health and simple remedies for illness. In 1747, he published a little book called *Primitive Physic*. This handbook for health became as indispensable for health care in his day as Dr. Spock's book was for raising children in the late twentieth century. *Primitive Physic* went through numerous additions, and was a bestseller on both sides of the Atlantic. In it, Wesley listed remedies for illnesses that had been handed down for generations.

He gave two or three remedies for each illness and suggested that if one did not work, try another. The book also gave simple rules for good health that are important in all times and places. They included clean fresh air, cleanliness and hygiene, exercise, adequate rest and sleep. He placed strong emphasis on exercise, advocating walking as the best exercise one could do. *Primitive Physic* was strong on healthcare basics. Because it was written for the poor, it focused on common household substances and natural means.

Wesley was as fascinated by electricity as Benjamin Franklin was, though he tended to use it in ways different from those of Franklin. Wesley somehow got his hands on an "electrifying apparatus," which he used in healing. The machine is now on display in Wesley's home near City Road Chapel in London. It is a small device, which could be packed into a hamper and carried on horseback. It is hard to see how it worked, just from looking at it, but it somehow passed a weak electrical current between two points. Wesley used it on himself to deal with the soreness after a fall from a horse. In fact, a weak electrical current could have helped relax stiff muscles and to give him relief. Not everyone, of course, was as thrilled with this machine as John himself. John was in a huff at one point when his brother Charles refused to be "electrified." Whatever the medical value of the machine—and it seems to have been useful in relaxing sore muscles, if nothing else—it does show that Wesley was willing to use the most up-to-date scientific knowledge and technology in his healthcare ministry. Certainly Wesley's attention to good habits kept him healthy until late in life when his body finally wore out.

WHAT WOULD HE SAY TO US?

John Wesley would be thrilled to see the great hospitals of the United States He would stand in awe at the miracles of modern surgery, ranging from simple appendectomies to heart-lung transplants. He would rejoice at the emphasis on medical research, the elimination of smallpox and polio, the attempt to find a vaccine for AIDS, and so on. The state of medical knowledge and the art of healing in his day were so primitive by our standards that he would fairly dance for joy at the sight of all that can be done today.

But he would also have a lot of questions. Why, he might ask, with all this knowledge and equipment and medication at your disposal, are so many without care? Why do so many babies die? Why do some have health insurance and others do not? Where in all your healing do you make room for God to work? Do you care for the whole person, or just for the affliction?

Wesley would also remind us that the key questions about medical care are not economic, or even scientific. The key questions are always religious. What does it take to bring wholeness to persons who are ill? What stands in the way of that wholeness? To what does God call the church in the field of health care?

QUESTIONS FOR REFLECTION

1. How are your own health habits? Do you eat a balanced diet? Exercise regularly? Keep a balance between your physical, emotional, and spiritual health?

2. Why are so many people in our society without adequate health care? Why do we have such high infant mortality rates? What are the underlying causes of the "health care crisis" in the United States? Read what The Social Principles have to say about health care. Then ask yourself, "what can I do? What could our congregation do?"

CHAPTER ELEVEN

What About God and Science?

One of the most commonly asked questions in confirmation by junior high students is about how to square the biblical story of creation with what they learn about evolution in school. "What about God and evolution?" That is also a common question among adults. One of the great controversies of our time is (yet once again) the perennial one about science and the Bible. Several states have required that science teachers teach creationism or intelligent design, side by side with evolution. In at least one state, creationism was first mandated, then dropped, then mandated again, depending on the election victory or defeat of certain individuals for the state board of education. The controversy is hot enough when the topic is evolution in general; when the topic is the evolution of humans, tempers flare and accusations fly back and forth. Evolution is, of course, not the only science topic about which there is controversy, but it is the model for the conversation between faith and science.

Other questions about science abound. For example, did we really put men on the moon, or was that all a clever hoax, perpetrated in a television studio on earth? More serious are questions such as, when does life begin? This has tremendous implications for topics such as abortion, stem-cell research, and related topics in both science and religion. Court cases rage around the question of the end of life, as well. Should persons who are kept alive only by machines be allowed to die? In its simplified form, this is a question about "the right to die." But it also has implications about the meaning of life, free will, and other issues not related directly to the basic medical question.

In many cases, biologists, physicists, medical professionals, for example, would love to have some ethical and philosophical guidance from the church on issues related to their research. Their cries for help often go unheeded for at least two reasons. First, "the church" does not speak with one voice, as in the public debate over stem-cell research. Second, most theologians and ethicists do not know enough about the science involved to respond to the questions about ethics. So the divide between science and religious faith continues, and widens, in many cases.

Science in Wesley's Day

The eighteenth century was a time of ferment and excitement on the frontiers of scientific knowledge. During Wesley's lifetime, the following advancements in basic science occurred.

> Sir Isaac Newton, the great theoretical physicist and "discoverer" of gravity, became President of the Royal Society in 1703, the year Wesley was born.
>
> Sir Edmund Halley published his *Synopsis on Cometary Astronomy* in 1705.

Gabriel Fahrenheit developed the temperature scale named after him in 1714.

In 1715, the calculus of finite differences was invented.

Stephen Hales measured blood pressure for the first time in 1726.

James Hutton was born in 1726. Hutton was one of the greatest geologists in England's history. Using empirical methods, he mapped the rock strata of England. He also helped develop the theory of "uniformitarianism" in geology.

Carolus Linnaeus published *Genera plantarum*, the beginning of the modern classification of plants, in 1737.

The Celsius scale for measuring temperature was developed in 1742.

The Leyden Jar, an electric condensor, was developed in 1745.

The first geological map of France was published in 1746.

In 1748, the first chair of astronomy was established at Cambridge.

Joseph Black "discovered" carbon dioxide in 1754.

In 1759 John Harrison developed the first accurate nautical chronometer, which was the key to accurately determining longitude.

Lomonosov detected the atmosphere on Venus in 1761.

Henry Cavendish "discovered" hydrogen in 1766.

In 1768, James Cook made his first voyage to the Pacific. One of the goals of his expedition was the discovery and classification of plants and animals then unknown to the European world.

Joseph Priestly discovered that plants release oxygen in 1771.

Daniel Rutherford distinguished between nitrogen and carbon dioxide in 1772.

James Herschel discovered Uranus in 1781.

In 1789, the element uranium was isolated and identified.

So what can we learn from that list? First, there were advances in research in chemistry, zoology, botany, physics, geology, astronomy, and medicine, at least. Second, the advances were not based on philosophical theories as in the past, but in direct observation and careful experiment.

As it turns out, Wesley was fascinated by science and its applications. We have already seen (in chapter 10) his interest in electricity and its potential applications in the field of medicine. But what did he think about our main interest—the relationship between science and religion?

IT COMES DOWN TO THE BIBLE

For Wesley, as for us, a key question was the relationship between science and Scripture. And here we need to step back and take a brief look at Scripture studies in the eighteenth century. This was the beginning of the modern period in religious thought, and Wesley was right in the middle of it. Because of his emphasis on reason, Methodism has sometimes been called the "first church of the Enlightenment." In the eighteenth century, the authority of the Bible was called into question as never before. Whereas for the Lutheran Reformers of an earlier period, Scripture was everything, the thinkers of the eighteenth century began to ask more and more questions about it. Even those who took the authority of the Bible as a given began see the Bible in a different way.

To anticipate Wesley's use of Scripture (Chapter 15), we can say that, for him, Scripture was sufficient for faith and practice, as the Articles of the Church of England said. He is clear that, on other matters, Scripture is not the supreme authority, though he seldom says so directly. For example, he takes for granted the results of scientific investigation, even when those results contradict the literal meaning of Scripture. For example, he published an abridgment of an earlier work as "A Survey of the Wisdom of God in Creation." In that work, he clearly accepts the results of the work of Galileo, Kepler, Copernicus, and others about the cosmos. Their observations and studies showed that the earth was not the center of what we now call the solar system, with the sun revolving around it, but that the sun itself was the center and the earth did the revolving. The scientific data had the depth of observation and the simplest explanation for all the observed phenomena. To defend the biblical notion that the earth was the center was to deny plain fact. So Wesley interpreted Scripture's authority on matters of science to mean that a geocentric view was what people saw, not necessarily what really is. He does not question that the earth moves around the sun. At the same time he says that Joshua 10:12-14 (where Joshua commands the sun to stand still) is to be taken literally (sermon "On Divine Providence"). In that sermon, he says that God made the sun stand still, and that this was a miracle precisely because it violates "the general laws of nature." On another issue, he does not argue against Newton's description of gravity as a natural law. Rather, he rejoices that the scientific description explains the ways of God.

Wesley was interested in science and he was guided by the empirical method of his day, not by proofs from Scripture. Indeed, he interpreted Scripture in the light of science. He was not interested in theories, but in description. Causes, or broad explanations of events were not his concern. What he was concerned with was facts, data that the mind could grasp. At the same time, he looked at the facts as ways of describing God's work, as well as describing the world around us. Where the results of science conflicted with the Bible, Wesley gave up the literal meaning of the biblical text—because the Bible was not intended to teach scientific truth!

So scientific facts about the heavens, for example, are not dependent on Scriptural authority. When Scripture makes claims about the world that science has disproved, Scripture must then be interpreted in a non-literal way. One wonders, in that light, what Wesley might have said about the age of the earth and the evolution of life, if he had had at his disposal the data of modern scientific findings. What would he have said about the earth being 4.5 *billion* years old, instead of some 6,000 years, as many in his day believed? What would he have said about creation taking all those years, instead of happening in six days? Or what about the development of life? What would he have said, if he had seen the data, about the rich fossil record for the development of life, spanning hundreds of millions of years? What would he have said about the much sparser, but no less fascinating, fossil record of the development of humans? Would he have said that Genesis 1 and 2 need to be interpreted in a non-literal way? We have no way of knowing, definitively, what he might have said. In the light of the way he interpreted Scripture in relationship to the scientific data of his own day, however, we can guess he might have said, "Yes, we need to re-interpret Genesis 1 and 2." In fact, in one of his early sermons, "The Image of God," Wesley speculated on how Adam eating the forbidden fruit could cause his death. It is clear from what he says in that sermon, that he completely accepted the physiology of his day, based on Harvey's proof of the circulation of the blood. It is clear from this sermon that Wesley was using the best of contemporary science to understand the Scripture and make it relevant to his listeners.

We will return to this point in Chapter 15, when we explore Wesley's interpretation of Scripture. Since most of what we know of Wesley's dealings with science relate to his interpretation of Scripture, however, it seemed important to include those understandings here, as well.

AND THE POINT OF ALL THIS IS?

What can we learn from Wesley's understandings of the science of his day to help us deal with the findings of science in our day?

Scripture is about faith and practice, not about science. Indeed, Wesley was clear that if science and Scripture are in contradiction, we need to interpret Scripture in non-literal ways. We'll turn to this again in Chapter 15.

The findings of science can help us understand Scripture, as well as the world around us.

When we talk about science and religion, we need to use the very best science we can. This is an inference from what Wesley said, but it seems to be a fair one. If we're going to debate creationism and evolution, for example, we need to know everything we can about the science of evolution before we begin. Or, again, in the current debates about stem-cell research, the church seems to be operating out of an *a priori* understanding that says any use of embryonic stem cells is murder and cannot be allowed. Now, that may very well be true, but we don't know enough about the beginning of life to be able to say so definitively. We need to know far more about the science of life before we make that kind of definitive statement about the ethics of stem-cell research.

Science can open our eyes to the wonder of God's world.

Don't "check your brains at the door" when you begin to struggle with questions about science and the faith.

QUESTIONS FOR REFLECTION

1. Listen carefully to discussions about science in your congregation. How often are people guided by *a priori* assumptions about the Bible, or about faith ideas, to the point where they aren't even willing to look at scientific data? What do you think Wesley would have said about an approach like that?

2. We talk a great deal about "finding God in nature." But how often do we build on the findings of science to deepen our appreciation of nature. For example, when you look at some of the pictures from the Hubble Space Telescope (on the birth of stars, for example), do you see God at work? Or, when you read about discoveries of new fossils that might be human ancestors, do you see God's hand in shaping humanity?

FOR FURTHER READING

Scott J. Jones, *John Wesley's Conception and Use of Scripture* (Nashville: Abingdon Press, 1995). Jones' work lays out in detail how Wesley interpreted Scripture. At several key points in the book, he details the points about science outlined above.

CHAPTER TWELVE

The Shame of a Nation

"My boss is such a slave driver. He reminds me of Dagwood's boss in the comics, Mr. What's-his name. Always yelling, piling on more work, never showing me any appreciation, making me work on weekends and at night."

"I've been slaving away all day, trying to make things nice for you. And you can't even say thanks?"

"I'm just a slave to the system. The only way to keep up my house, my cars, my kids' school and soccer and swimming and dance is to put in longer and longer hours."

All those people are using "slavery" as an exaggeration for hard work. The reality of slavery is a topic we want to avoid in the United States. It is the most painful memory in our national culture. The forced labor of African slaves was a crime against humanity, and a blot on our nation's honor. We fought a great war over slavery and, when the slaves were freed, we continued to hold them in economic bondage for nearly another century. The indenture of European servants was a form of slavery, and yet a notch above slavery, because at least those servants saw an end to their indenture. "Sweat shops" were, and are, a form of economic slavery. We'd rather not think about those awful parts of our past—and present, in some cases.

BUT SLAVERY IS A THING OF THE PAST, RIGHT?

Wrong. Slavery continues to flourish in our world today. People who are hungry, homeless, or otherwise vulnerable are lured into debt slavery because they are promised a better life. Some of them are forced into prostitution. Some are forced laborers. Some are illegal immigrants who pay large fees to an "agent," who smuggles them into a nation, and then keeps them in virtual slavery because of the debts run up. Some are children sold as jockeys, as prostitutes, as laborers. Some are farm laborers whose parents passed on debts to them and they will, in turn, pass those debts on their children. These represent some of the worst forms of the "company store," or sharecroppers, who can never get out of debt and can therefore never be free. All these people are desperate, seeking a better life. And this is not a third-world phenomenon. By some estimates, there are between 100,000 and 150,000 slaves in the United States today. (National Geographic, September, 2003, p. 23)

So, in spite of our living in the twenty-first century, in a time we consider enlightened, in a kinder, gentler, world, slavery still exists. What did John Wesley have to say about slavery? And what would he say to us?

SLAVERY IN THE EIGHTEENTH CENTURY

There were not many African slaves in England itself, but the agricultural economy of England's colonies in the New World depended heavily on the importation of slave laborers. Sugar in the West Indies, tobacco and cotton on the North American mainland, were labor-intensive crops, and plantation owners depended heavily on the importation of slaves to work their fields.

The English slave trade began in 1562, when Sir John Hawkins took three hundred slaves from Sierra Leone. At first, the slave trade by English slavers was to the Spanish colonies in the New World, but then England began developing its own empire there. By the beginning of the eighteenth century, England had a virtual monopoly on the slave trade. Between 1680 and 1786, 2,130,000 slaves were imported into British colonies, the vast majority for the sugar plantations. The conditions of the slaves were cruel and inhuman, but the primary motive of both plantation owners and slavers was profit, not humanitarianism.

WESLEY AND SLAVERY

Into this world came John Wesley. He learned about slavery first-hand during his stay in Georgia. General Oglethorpe did not allow African slaves to be imported into Georgia, but Wesley saw all he needed to see on trips to South Carolina. In Georgia, he supported Oglethorpe's policy. He also angered some of the leading colonists for attacking white slavery—the indenture system, which was essentially a system of debt slavery.

The young Wesley did not engage in a blanket condemnation of slavery. He opposed inhuman conditions, and was involved in pastoral concern for individual African slaves. In South Carolina, he talked to slaves, arranged preaching services for them, and taught them in the faith. He saw to it that slaves had the opportunity for education (a program that slave owners would soon stop). In his ministry, Wesley did not distinguish between whites and blacks. Slaves were admitted to baptism and Lord's Supper along with whites.

Wesley's return to England in 1738, of course, took him away from the heart of slave labor, though not from the heart of the slave trade. The seeds of later struggles against slavery had been planted in him in America, however, and would come to full flower after 1770.

In 1774, Wesley published his "Thoughts upon Slavery." His arguments against slavery were based not so much on Scripture and theology as on natural law and a sense of justice. In that treatise, he wrote, "I absolutely deny all slave-holding to be consistent with any degree of even natural justice." ("Thoughts upon Slavery," quoted in Bready, p. 225) He also attacked the attitude that saw Empire and patriotism only in terms of economics or geographical expansion. When he was reminded of the economic importance of the sugar plantations in the West Indies, he replied, "It is better that all these islands should remain uncultivated forever; yea, it were more desirable that they were all together sunk in the depth of the sea than that they should be cultivated at so high a price as the violation of justice, mercy, and truth." ("Thoughts upon Slavery," quoted in Bready, p. 225) He argued that slaveholding could not be brought into harmony with natural law, which left only economic necessity as a rationale. The argument was that black slaves were necessary, because whites could not stand to work in the heat. Wesley scoffed at that argument, saying whites could stand the heat as well as blacks. But his underlying theme was that slavery was a blow to fundamental human rights. Ignoring the rights of blacks degraded them and put them in a less-than-human social and moral position. For this degradation, Wesley argued, slave owners were fully responsible.

Now Wesley was, by birth and inclination, a social and political conservative. But his religious convictions turned him into a radical reformer whenever and wherever conservatism interfered with liberty and human progress. He attacked slave-owners, the captains of slave ships, slave merchants, and even the judges who upheld the legal right to own slaves. "Are there any laws as binding as the eternal laws of justice?" he asked in response to court rulings. Liberty, he argued is "the right of every human creature as soon as he breathes the vital air." ("Thoughts upon Slavery," quoted in Bready, p. 226) When he was told that English slave masters were more humane than the French or Dutch, Wesley was ready with the comeback that liberty and justice were not about degrees, but were absolute, and he attacked those who supported slavery for economic gain.

In "A Serious Address to the People of England with regard to the State of the Nation," written in 1777, he reacted to those who were moaning over the economic losses because the slave trade to the colonies had been stopped. "I would to God that it may never be found more. That we may never more steal and sell our brethren like beasts, never murder them by thousands and tens of thousands!" (Bready, p. 227)

The Conference of 1780 opposed slavery as "contrary to the laws of God, of man, and of nature, and injurious to the Society." (Marquardt, p. 72). That brief phrase encompasses natural law, the basic concepts of justice, theology, and economics, and finds slavery a wrong in every case. This statement, along with Wesley's writings, did stir up a protest that eventually led to the prohibition of slavery in England, and, ultimately, an end to the African slave trade.

Six days before his death, John Wesley wrote his last letter. It was to William Wilberforce, the Parliamentary leader in the fight against the slave trade. In that brief letter, he said, "Oh, be not weary in well doing. Go on, in the name of God, and in the power of His might, until even American slavery, the vilest that ever saw the sun, shall vanish away before it." (Bready, p. 228)

To the last, Wesley was fighting against injustice and evil, in the name of God.

BACK TO SLAVERY TODAY

One wonders, to what extent does the economy of the United States depend on some form of slavery, whether it is debt slavery, sweat shops, or other forms of bondage and injustice? Should we be concerned about child slavery in much of the world? About women forced into prostitution? Or laborers in virtual slavery because of generations of debt? Would Wesley say to us, as he said to Wilberforce, "Go on, in the name of God, and in the power of his might until (every vestige of) slavery" shall vanish away? What does our Christian faith, our understanding of God and salvation in our Wesleyan heritage, suggest to us about opposition to slavery?

QUESTIONS FOR REFLECTION

1. Were you aware that slavery still exists in our world today? Do a quick internet search to see how much you can find out about slavery.

2. Wesley said that liberty and justice were not about degrees, but about absolutes. What did he mean by that? What arguments could you make on both sides of that statement? Is morality a relative or an absolute? Are there times when Christians must take a stand on the absolutes? And are there times when we need to settle for a relative good, in order to keep the way open for more progress later? What do you think?

FOR FURTHER READING

Manfred Marquardt, *John Wesley's Social Ethics.* (Nashville: Abingdon Press, 1992).

Warren Thomas Smith, *John Wesley and Slavery* (Nashville: Abingdon Press, 1986).

Andrew Cockburn, "21st-Century Slaves," and Lynne Warren "Inhuman Profit," *National Geographic* (September 2003) pages 2–29.

CHAPTER THIRTEEN

A Love-Hate Relationship— Politics

"No, I didn't even bother to vote. Everything in Washington is run by the lobbyists, anyway. No one cares about a little guy like me. Besides, I'm too busy."

"Is the government the solution, or the problem?" That bumper sticker may sum up the feelings of most Americans about the government and political life in general. Does the government actually have the power to solve the problems of our society, or is it, in fact, the problem? How one answers that question determines almost everything else about one's participation in the political process. I recently overhead a conversation in which one of the participants asked, rather wistfully, can't we even agree on how much government we need?

"Can you really trust _____?" (Put the name of your least favorite candidate here.)

In the 2004 Presidential race, faith and religion played a role larger than at any time since John F. Kennedy, a Roman Catholic, met with the Houston, TX, Ministerial Alliance to convince them he would not allow the Pope to dictate United States policy. One candidate in the 2004 election was a "born-again" Christian who talked freely and easily about his faith. The other was a Roman Catholic, who was less comfortable talking about his faith publicly, but was serious about practicing it. All through the campaign, there were debates, essays, and editorials about the role of faith in politics, and the extent to which faith could be a marker in a nation that is committed, constitutionally, to a separation of church and state.

Which leads us to the question of religion and politics. How do they mix in our society? And does John Wesley have any words of wisdom for us on this topic?

IT'S ANOTHER WORLD

Wesley lived in a world far different from ours. England was ruled by a king. Parliament was growing in power, and England was becoming more and more a constitutional monarch, true. But there was still a strong strain in English politics, including in John Wesley, which believed in the divine right of kings. They believed that George III, for example, ruled by divine right, because God had chosen him King. To go against the King was to go against the will of God. You rightly suspect that the colonists in New England and Virginia had some different thoughts about the relationship between George III and God!

That was Wesley's world. The King ruled through ministers, who were chosen by the dominant party in Parliament. Voting for members of Parliament was restricted to a minority of the population, and certainly not an option for the poor among whom Wesley ministered. In addition, Wesley was a Tory by birth and inclination. The Tories were the conservative party in English politics in the eighteenth century, just as they are today. Loyalty to the King and the King's ministers were, for Wesley, an important part of his religion.

In Wesley's day, there was a strong suspicion that the Tories were Jacobites, that is, that they wanted to restore the Stuart kings (Bonnie Prince Charlie, and all that crowd) to power. For most of his life, Wesley had to defend himself against charges of being a Jacobite.

Wesley *said* that he saw himself as having no political role. In 1782, he published an essay called "How Far Is It the Duty of a Christian Minister to Preach Politics?" One would think this would be a clear definition of the situation and solve the question of Wesley's political involvement forever. Unfortunately, he confines the preaching of politics to defending the King, and the King's ministers, against slanders and lies. Three times in this short essay (less than two pages), he says that the chief business of the clergy is to preach Christ, and Christ crucified. That seems to sum up Wesley's attitude toward the political system. That attitude is almost a hands-off one. Don't bother with politics, except to set the record straight when people lie about the King or the King's ministers.

Wesley did advise Methodist voters about voting. He told them they should vote morally, that is, they should not accept bribes or other favors in return for their votes. In addition, he said, they should vote for the candidate that "loves God". If there were no candidate who loves God, then they should vote for the one who supports King George. That's a pretty direct statement, in terms of telling people how to vote! The first part, about voting for the candidate who loves God, raises more problems than it solves. How does one determine which candidate loves God? How much weight should campaign rhetoric bear in answering that question? How does one determine the relative weight of words and deeds?

In spite of denying any role in politics, Wesley felt free to intervene in politics for the sake of moral and political issues. One such intervention was the fight against slavery, as we saw in Chapter 12. From 1768 to 1778, he became increasingly involved in the American struggles over taxation and representation. As a staunch conservative, Wesley was not moved by calls for democracy and "the rights of Englishmen." In theoretical terms, Wesley denied that government was somehow a "contract" with the people. The idea of contract, or covenant, was a key element of the Puritan Revolution in England, and found its way into both the Declaration of Independence and the Constitution of the United States. (Though not always in that language.) Wesley believed that people had never chosen their own rulers, but insisted that power was from God, and those to whom God gave it (i.e., the rightful king). In his "Calm Address to the American Colonies" (which was anything but calm!), Wesley argued against the idea that there could be no taxation without representation. After all, he said, that's the situation for most Englishmen. This pamphlet caused all kinds of upheaval in the colonies, and forced all but one of the English Methodist preachers to return to England. (The exception was Francis Asbury, who was the "father" of American Methodism.)

All through his life, Wesley leaned on the biblical idea of obedience to the powers that be. See Romans 13 for an expression of this idea.

NOW I'M MORE CONFUSED THAN BEFORE

Would John Wesley want me, and other United Methodists, to just go along with whoever is in the White House and Congress and never say anything against them? What do I do if I think the President, or the Congress, is leading us down a wrong path? Can't I protest against that, as a citizen?

Certainly Wesley would say to us that we should obey the

government that is set over us. He would argue that on biblical grounds. We might argue it on the grounds of corporate calm, and the importance of peaceful transfers of power. Wesley would also say that we have the right, even the obligation, to work to influence the government, to work for changes in public policy that are for the common good. He would remind us how easy it is to confuse our own desires with the common good, and warn us to not be certain that we are doing God's will in opposing the government (and we might add, in supporting it). He would want us to remember that we have the obligation to vote, without taking any bribes or other inducements, and that we should vote for the candidate whom we believe "loves God". In our day, we have to do some serious thinking about what that means.

There are radical differences between our political situation and Wesley's. We have universal suffrage, a vote not limited to a relative handful. We don't have a king (or queen) who is the symbol of unity for our nation; rather we have two dominant political parties, and whichever one is in office is attacked by the party out of office. The head of our state changes every four to eight years. We live in a nation that is committed, by our Constitution, and by the common interpretations of that Constitution, to a separation of church and state. For Wesley, the King, the government, and the Church of England were one and the same.

So, in the political arena, we have to admit there are not many Wesleyan guidelines to follow. But we can learn from his deep sense of the need for morality in government, and morality in the way we vote. We can pray and seek to discern God's will as we understand it and to use that discernment to vote and to seek to influence our politicians. We can learn from Wesley that we have the right to work to influence government. Wesley would warn us to be humble about confusing our own political opinions with the will of God. And, incredibly important for a time when only a small majority of eligible voters actually do vote, Wesley would urge us to get to the polls!

QUESTIONS FOR REFLECTION

1. What is your personal attitude toward government? What is your personal commitment to morality in the political process?

2. How informed are you on the key political issues of your day? Is it important for you to be informed?

3. How regularly do you vote? Do you think it matters if you vote in every election you can?

4. How do you attempt to influence the government? Do you write to your representatives? Contribute financially? Participate in protest groups? Why do you do any of those things?

CHAPTER FOURTEEN

War and Peace

In the author's lifetime, the United States has been engaged in these wars·

> World War II
>
> Korea
>
> The Cold War
>
> Vietnam
>
> The invasions of Grenada and Panama
>
> The Gulf War of 1991
>
> Somalia
>
> The invasion of Afghanistan, and
>
> The invasion of Iraq.

In addition, we have supplied weapons and troops to count-less "brush fires" and "training missions" in places such as the Philippines, Colombia, Yemen, and on and on. We live in a time of almost constant war. That is not a judgment, but a statement of fact. And we, as citizens, disagree about our nation's involve-ment in at least some of those wars. That, too, is a statement of fact. This chapter will not take a position on any of those wars, or on the role of the United States as a superpower in a post-cold war world. Rather, it will look at John Wesley's thoughts on war, to see what we can learn from him for our own day.

WESLEY'S THOUGHTS ON WAR

We saw, in Chapter 6, the long list of wars in which England fought during the eighteenth century. This was the period when England was becoming a major world power, and extending its rule over more and more of the globe. Even though the American colonies were lost, England held on to Canada, and added India to the Empire. For most of Wesley's life, there were Englishmen fighting and dying somewhere around the world, if not in Europe itself. So what did he think on the subject of war?

For all his conservatism, and his loyalty to King and coun-try, Wesley was not fond of war. He did not leap to the notion that we have to support the ruler in time of war, no matter what. His writings on war, specifically the war that we call the American Revolution, tended to blame both sides equally.

The most extended writing on war is found in his essay, "The Doctrine of Original Sin," which was published in 1756, during what we call the French and Indian War, which was actu-ally the first of several world wars fought between the English and the French. The goal of both sides in these wars was expanded colonies, trade opportunities (and monopolies) and economic power. Here's what Wesley had to say about the causes of war at his sarcastic best:

But is there not a cause? O yes: "The causes of war," as the same writer observes," are innumerable. Some of the chief are these: The ambition of Princes; or the corruption of their Ministers: Difference of opinion; as, whether flesh be bread or bread be flesh; whether the juice of the grape be blood or wine; what is the best colour for a coat, whether black, white, or grey; and whether it should be long or short, whether narrow or wide. Nor are there any wars so furious as those occasioned by such difference of opinions." (*Works*, IX, p. 221)

Wesley goes on to list other causes, such as the desire for more territory, the desire for power over a weaker country, or what we would call a pre-emptive strike, to make war on a stronger neighbor who might not be prepared at present, but whom a king dares not allow become stronger.

But it is the result of war that most bothers Wesley and calls forth some of his most eloquent prose.

But whatever the cause, let us calmly and impartially consider the thing itself. Here are forty thousand men gathered together on this plain. What are they going to do? See, there are thirty or forty thousand more at a little distance. And these are going to shoot them through the head or body, to stab them, or split their skulls, and send most of their souls into everlasting fire, as fast as they possibly can. Why so? What harm have they done to them? O none at all! They do not so much as know them. But a man, who is King of France, has a quarrel with another man, who is King of England. So these Frenchmen are to kill as many of these Englishmen as they can, to prove the King of France is in the right. Now, what an argument is this! What a method of proof! What an amazing way of deciding controversies! What must mankind be, before such a thing as war could even be known or thought of upon earth? (*Works*, IX, p. 222)

The context of those passages is, as noted, an essay on original sin. Wesley saw original sin as the nature of the human spirit apart from God, and war is only one of several examples he uses to illustrate the point. For him, war is an expression of sin, of life lived without God in the world. The causes of war he lists (and there are more in the original essay) are all examples of the self-centeredness, short-sightedness, and willful disobedience to God that are the marks of sin.

Wesley is clear that war cannot be reconciled to religion. But more than that—war cannot be reconciled to any degree of reason, or of common sense. Think about it. What is reasonable about sending young men (and women as well, in our day) off to war? Where is the common sense in that? In another ironic passage, Wesley expresses amazement that, in the slaughter and destruction of war, we can still talk about human dignity. We can't do that, he says. We can't talk about the power of human reason, so long as there is war in the world.

In May of 1775, Wesley wrote a letter to Thomas Rankin, who was head of the Methodist missionaries in America. At this point, war between England and the colonies seemed almost inevitable. In that letter Wesley wrote; "wherever war breaks out, God is forgotten." (*Works*, 12, p. 327) A major concern for Wesley was that war would lead people to forget God, overcome by waves of patriotism, anger, fear, despair, and the physical suffering brought on by war.

Also in 1775, this time in November, Wesley preached a sermon called "National Sins and Miseries." In the sermon, he explored the causes of the war with America. These included the loss of freedom of speech, freedom of the press, and civil liberties in the colonies. He was sympathetic with the grievances of the colonists, but still did not think these grievances were reasons for war. War, he said, would only compound the problem. The sermon does not really take sides, but focuses on the folly of both sides in moving toward war. It's interesting that, even though Wesley was not interested in politics and preached loyalty to the king and his ministers (see chapter 13) he points out to those ministers the folly of going to war.

Finally, in 1776, he published a little tract called "A

Seasonable Address to the More Serious Part of the Inhabitants of Great Britain" (and that's the condensed version of the title!). Instead of publishing it over his own name, he wrote on the title page, By a Lover of Peace. In the essay, he pointed out the stupidity of what was getting ready to happen in the colonies. Englishmen (on both sides) were going to kill each other, to prove who is right on the question of taxation without representation! He was amazed at the waste and stupidity involved in making major decisions on the basis of "who can lick whom." He was not interested in who was right, or who "started it," only in the waste involved in war. Surely, he argued, there are better ways of solving disagreements than this.

At about the same time, he was writing to Rankin in America, expressing a hope that the preachers could work for peace between the two sides, and war could be averted through their efforts.

And yet, Wesley was not a pacifist. He thought war was foolish and wasteful, and there should be better ways of solving international disputes. It is not clear if he believed in Augustine's "just war" theory. In fact, already by Wesley's day, it was almost impossible to meet the requirements of a "just war" laid down over 1300 years before. But when it seemed that France might invade England, Wesley proclaimed his support for the government, and even offered to raise a regiment for the defense of the homeland. As in so many other areas, Wesley was an amazingly complex person when it came to the thorny questions of war and peace.

In one of his essays on the causes of poverty, and the lack of food for the poor, Wesley did advocate cutting the size of the army, in order to make grain available for the poor. That statement shows that, like all the rest of us, Wesley did not always think through what he was saying. If the King had actually disbanded regiments and used the savings to provide grain for the poor, the law of unintended consequences would have kicked in. All those discharged soldiers would have been without work, and in need of the same grain that Wesley intended for the poor. Chances are that the situation of the poor would not have improved in that case. But, the idea does suggest that Wesley was willing to consider serious change in government policy in order to care for the needs of the poor.

AND WE HAVE LEARNED . . . ?

Questions about war and peace are never easy for Christians. We live in the tension between loving our neighbors, even loving our enemies, on the one hand, and the desire to be loyal citizens of a nation we love, on the other. This tension has always divided the church, and our generation is no exception. But what can we learn from Wesley about war that we can make a part of our lives today?

First, there is the awareness of the horrors of war. Remember Wesley's description of the armies killing each other. Add to that the so-called "collateral damage," the deaths and wounding of civilians, the destruction of the infrastructure of the warring nations, and the devastation of economies. As General Sherman said, "war is hell," even when it is necessary.

Second, I think Wesley would want us to remember that God's ultimate will is peace. One of the implications of that is to look carefully at the reasons for war. Obviously, if a nation is attacked, it will defend itself. The list above of some of the reasons why nations go to war reminds us that we often do not look for God's ultimate will, or even for a common-sense reason for war. Instead, we focus on selfish ends, the expressions of what Wesley called original sin.

Third, Wesley's statement that, in war, God is forgotten is a powerful one. The old adage says that there are no atheists in foxholes. That may or may not be true. It does seem to be true, however, that God's ultimate will is easily forgotten in time of war.

QUESTIONS FOR REFLECTION

1. Think about your own position on war. What do you believe is an adequate justification for going to war?

2. What do you think about Wesley's statement that war is contrary to reason and common sense? Why would he say something like that? What reasons can you think of that might make that statement true for our time?

3. Wesley said that war was an expression of original sin. What do you think he meant by that? Can you think of examples in our time when that might be true?

4. What do you think about Wesley's comment that God is forgotten in war?

5. Sing or read "Let Us Plead for Faith Alone, (*The United Methodist Hymnal* #385) or "Jesus, Thine All-Victorious Love," (*The United Methodist Hymnal* # 422). How do you relate these hymns to war and peace?

CHAPTER FIFTEEN

Scripture, and Scripture Alone, But . . .

"Do you believe that the Bible is the word of God?"

"Yes, but I want you to stop and listen to what I mean when I say that."

"I don't care about all your little ways to deny the truth. Do you believe that the Bible is the word of God?"

"OK, so we know we can't believe everything the Bible says. How do we know what we're supposed to believe?"

When the Revised Standard Version of the Old Testament was first published in 1952, many pastors took it into the pulpit and ripped out the page that contained Isaiah 7:14. Why? Because the new translation said "a young woman shall conceive," instead of "a virgin shall conceive," as in the King James. In this case, doctrine trumped a more accurate translation.

"You can prove anything by the Bible." That's true, if you take verses out of context. And many of us do that. We find a verse that, by itself, makes the point we want to make. So we quote it, as if it were the full and only truth. Only, many times, when we look at the verse in its full context, we find it doesn't mean what the argument seems to say it does.

What do we do about the Bible? What kind of authority does it have? Is it really the inspired word of God? How do we understand and interpret the Bible?

JOHN WESLEY ON SCRIPTURE

John Wesley was a complex person, and his thought was as complex as the rest of his personality. He said, "Let me be *homo unius libri*" (a man of one book), by which he meant he wanted to ground everything in the Bible. But, in the same sermon where he said that, he quoted from the Greek classics. Wesley read everything, and used what he read in his preaching, his writing, and his teaching. He read devotional classics, theology, the Fathers of the early church, science, history.

He urged his followers to read widely, as well.

When Wesley set the American church free to organize separately from him, he sent a shortened version of the Articles of Religion (of the Church of England) for use in America. That version still remains as one of the bedrock doctrinal standards of United Methodism. Article V is titled, "Of the Sufficiency of the Holy Scriptures for Salvation," and reads in part:

> The Holy Scripture containeth all things necessary to salvation; so that whatsoever is not read therein, nor may be proved thereby, is not to be required of any man that it should be believed as an article of faith, or be thought requisite or necessary to salvation.
>
> (*The Book of Discipline*, 1996 edition, p. 58)

Since Wesley sent this to America unchanged from the Articles of the Church of England, we can feel confident it reflects his thought about the Bible. What does it say to us? First, the Bible "contains all things necessary to salvation." We don't have to go looking for God's plan of salvation anywhere else. If someone comes along with a new idea about salvation that is not compatible with Scripture, we don't have to take it seriously, or believe that it is necessary for salvation. Second, and equally important, is what the article does *not* say. It does not say that the Bible contains all truth in all topics for all time. Wesley did not believe that the Bible was a textbook for history, or biology, or geology, or astronomy, for example. In the chapter on science, we saw that he was open to the Copernican view of the universe, and applied that view to his understanding of the Scripture. He interpreted the Bible in the light of science, and not the other way around. In Chapter 1, when we looked at Wesley's spirituality, we saw his outline of a "grand scheme of salvation" (pages 13-16). This is what he meant when he said the Scripture contains all things necessary to salvation. On those biblical doctrines he stood firm. Other parts of the Bible he was willing to interpret in the light of knowledge from other disciplines.

So Wesley did not believe that Scripture was inerrant, that is, that it was never wrong. Nor did he think that all parts of the Bible were equally binding on Christians. For example, he identified three kinds of law in the Old Testament—moral, ceremonial, and political. It is clear that he thought the ceremonial and political laws were written for specific historical and religious situations that no longer existed. Therefore, they were not binding on Christians in his time (or, by extension, in our time). The moral law, however, was timeless, and binding on all the people of God, in all times and places. So there are degrees, or levels, of understanding the authority of Scripture. So does that mean the Scripture has no authority? For Wesley, the

Scripture was authoritative, just not on all subjects.

SCRIPTURE AS A MEANS OF GRACE

John Wesley clearly saw the Bible as a means of grace, that is, as a way in which we come to know God and God's love for us, find guidance and meaning for our lives, and grow in our faith. He was also aware that it is difficult for many Christians to just open the Bible and find meaning and faith. Although he sometimes practiced that kind of random opening of the Bible, he was more interested in a careful reading and meditation approach. So how do we read the Bible?

We begin, Wesley says, with prayer. We pray to be open to God's word in the Bible; we pray that God's Spirit will enlighten our minds as we read. This was an important theological point for Wesley, as well as a practical one. He believed that the Spirit who inspired the writing of the Scripture also inspired the understanding of those who read it centuries later. Prayer, then, is the key to really understanding the Bible.

Wesley is a bit vague on *how* the Spirit works to help us understand Scripture. He just takes for granted that this happens. Sometimes, he says, the Spirit may help us remember events or relationships. These events/relationships could help us understand more clearly what the Bible says. Or, the Bible could help us understand those events/relationships more clearly. (As in, "Oh, so that's what God was doing there.") Sometimes the Spirit convicts us of sin as we read the Scripture. That is, the Spirit helps us see a part of our life in an entirely new light—we now see that what we thought was innocuous, or even good, was really a sin against God and/or our neighbor. Sometimes the Spirit opens the Scripture to us like a ray of sunshine on a dark, gloomy day, bringing us hope and salvation and joy in the midst of our despair.

Wesley also was convinced that the Spirit worked with our

reason to help us understand Scripture and how it relates to our life. Remember, in the Wesleyan tradition, we don't have to check our brains at the door. God calls us to use the wonderful gift of reason to help us grow to a deeper faith and richer life.

Scott Jones, in his *John Wesley's Conception and Use of Scripture*, pulls from various places in Wesley's writings a list of principles of interpretation. Below you will find the list, along with some comments on how we might apply each of the principles in our own use of the Bible.

> Speak as the oracles of God.
>
> Use the literal sense unless it contradicts another Scripture or implies an absurdity.
>
> Interpret the text with regard to its literary context.
>
> Scripture interprets Scripture, according to the analogy of faith and by parallel passages.
>
> Commandments are covered promises.
>
> Interpret literary devices appropriately.
>
> Seek the most original text and the best translation. (Jones, p. 110)

Let's look at these briefly, beginning with the last. The basic principle of Biblical interpretation is finding the translation that most faithfully reproduces the original text. Remember that Wesley read the Bible in Hebrew and Greek, so he was a pretty good judge of accurate translations. Since we no longer have any of the original manuscripts of the Bible, this depends on following centuries of biblical scholarship. For the Old Testament, there is a scholarly consensus that the biblical manuscripts found among the Dead Sea Scrolls represent the most original. This includes the scroll of Isaiah that led to the controversies over the Revised Standard Version. In practical terms, Wesley would want us to consider (it seems to me) the relative value of a good *translation*, as opposed to a paraphrase. That is, in his terms, the New Revised Standard Version or the New International Version would have a higher relative value than The Message or The Living Bible, because they are more faithful translations of the most original texts.

Context is an important key to understanding. We all know, in a variety of settings, how sentences can be ripped out of context and made to mean something entirely different from what the writer meant. Context can be as simple as the paragraph in which a sentence is found, or as wide-ranging as the whole of Scripture. We need to consider historical context. When was this book written? What was the historical situation? How does the history affect the way we understand the message? The literary context is important. What kind of literature is this? Is it an historical narrative, a poem, a collection of wise sayings, or a letter? We read each of those genres differently, and this also affects the way we understand what we read. What is the cultural context? That is, what elements in the culture of the time do we need to understand in order to grasp the full meaning of a passage? We don't carry all that information in our heads when we sit down to read the Bible, so we refer to commentaries, Bible dictionaries, or Bible handbooks to help us understand what we're reading. Using our reason is an important part of understanding the Bible.

Closely related to context is the importance of interpreting literary devices appropriately. The Bible is rich in metaphors and similes, which are not meant to be taken literally. To use a non-biblical example, when we read that a mother heard her baby crying and flew upstairs to see what was the matter, we don't take that to mean that the mother sprouted wings and floated up the stairway. In the same way, when we read Jesus' words, "I am the vine," we don't think of him as a grapevine, with tendrils and leaves. But other metaphors and rhetorical devices are more subtle, and we have to read carefully.

Of all Wesley's principles of interpretation, the statement that "commandments are covered promises" is one of the richest. By that he meant that commandments are really promises of God about what we can become. For example, in the Beatitudes, Jesus says all these things that seem impossible for anyone to really live out. We have two choices on how we interpret those, Wesley says. We can see them as law and despair, because we know we can never live up to them. Or, we can see them as promises and rejoice, because God fulfills what God promises. This reflects Wesley's basic concern for holy living. This is how God calls us to live. God expects this of us. But God has also promised that, in Christ, we can live this way. So the commandments really are gospel and not law. Other commandments that we might take seriously as covered promises include Exodus 20:1-18, Matthew 22:37-40, Matthew 5:48, and John 13:34.

When we don't understand a part of Scripture, it can often be understood by reference to another part of Scripture. Or, more likely, when we understand more and more of Scripture, the vague passages become clear when we see them in the light of the entire Bible. And, again, sometimes we have to understand a particular passage in the light of the "analogy of faith," which is another term Wesley uses for the grand plan of salvation. That is, the key to Scripture is that plan of salvation (see Chapter 1), and we can interpret unclear passages in the light of the "plan."

DID WESLEY REALLY HAVE A "QUADRILATERAL"?

In a report for the 1972 General Conference, Dr. Albert Outler of Perkins School of Theology outlined what he called the "Wesleyan Quadrilateral," a fourfold way of doing theology, based on Scripture, tradition, reason, and experience. This caused a major furor in the church and was later changed to talk about the "primacy of Scripture," interpreted by tradition, reason, and experience. A part of the furor was the question, did Wesley really talk about the quadrilateral?

The answer is "no," in the sense that Wesley used the word, "quadrilateral". Nor does he ever talk about all four of those elements at the same time. He does however, talk about all four of them as important for understanding the Bible, and for developing faith. The ideas are still important for us today. We've already talked about the importance of Scripture for faith. Here we will look at tradition, reason, and experience, and how we use them as tools for understanding Scripture and faith.

Tradition, for Wesley, meant primarily the traditions of the early church and those of the Church of England. Wesley believed that what he called "the primitive church" was the most perfect expression of the church that had ever existed. So he relied heavily on the writings of the Church Fathers, the writers of that early period. In turn, he believed that the Church of England was the most perfect reflection, in his day, of the primitive church. So he appealed to the authority of both the Church of England and the Fathers in both theological and practical matters. For example, he appeals to St. John Chrysostom on justification by faith, and to others of the Eastern Fathers for his teachings on sanctification. When he finally gave in and ordained clergy for America, he did so on the grounds that, in the early church, priests could ordain other priests without the blessing of the bishop.

Reason was always important for Wesley. He was a child of the Enlightenment, as well as of the Church, and this always shows in his preaching and writing. He believed that God had given to humans a rational faculty, and called them to use it. However, reason had limitations for Wesley. He was not convinced that we can think our way into and through all issues. Reason is only a tool we use for discerning God's way in the world. Even with its limitations, however, reason is a powerful tool for the faith. One of the questions we ask about theological arguments is, "does that make sense?" Does it hang together with what we know of the Bible, the teachings of the church, and a broader range of knowledge in the humanities and sciences?

Experience, for Wesley, meant two things. First, he accepted the ideas of John Locke that all our ideas are based on experience. But he used experience primarily in a much narrower way, namely our religious experience. For him, religious experience was an objective reality, and therefore was a source of authority of Christian faith and life.

As principles of interpretation, tradition, reason, and experience continue to play an important role in our faith. We bring to our study of Scripture a wide range of experience. We bring a wide range of knowledge, from both the humanities and the sciences. We bring questioning minds. We bring an awareness that our religious experiences—the stories and prayers and songs we learned as children, and the values we inherited from our families—are powerful shapers of who we are and what we believe. All of those are a part of the process that we bring to the study of Scripture, and to the understanding of faith and life for the twenty-first century.

WHAT CAN I LEARN FROM WESLEY ABOUT TAKING THE BIBLE SERIOUSLY?

We have learned some surprising things about Wesley's approach to the Bible. He definitely believed it was *an* authority, even the most important authority, but there were also other authorities. He believed that both the writing and the reading of Scripture were inspired by the Spirit, but he did not believe the Scripture was inerrant. He believed the Bible contained everything we need to know about salvation, but that the Bible was not an equal authority in all realms of knowledge. Wesley took a very modern approach to studying and understanding the Bible, particularly in terms of the use of language and figures of speech, using the best possible translation, and bringing to bear the best of our reason, experience and tradition.

One thing Wesley *might* say to the people called United Methodists today would be to "chill." Don't get so upset and angry with each other over the Bible until you learn to take the Bible more seriously. Don't take the passages out of context and proclaim them as absolute truth. Don't use Bible passages as weapons against each other. Talk together in love and try to understand each other.

QUESTIONS FOR REFLECTION

1. What do you believe about the Bible? Did reading what Wesley believed about the Bible make sense to you? Were there "ah-ha" moments as you read? At what points did you disagree? Are you clear on *why* you disagree?

2. Look again at the points of understanding quoted from Jones' book. Are those guidelines you use for understanding the Bible? Which ones could you add to your Bible study?

3. How does Scripture help lead you to holy living?

FOR FURTHER READING

Scott J. Jones, *John Wesley's Conception and Use of Scripture.* (Nashville: Abingdon Press, 1995).

Scott J. Jones, *United Methodist Doctrine: The Extreme Center.* (Nashville: Abingdon Press, 2002).